FORGET JOB SECURITY

BUILD YOUR
MARKETABILITY!

FINDING JOB SUCCESS
IN THE NEW ERA
OF CAREER MANAGEMENT

DAWN RASMUSSEN

ISBN: 0615621201
ISBN-13: 9780615621203

Library of Congress Control Number: 2012905638
CreateSpace, North Charleston, SC

DEDICATION

To my husband, Brad Rasmussen, who supported me during my own career transition, Sydney Schultz (aka my godmother) who has always been there for me, my mother-in-law Sandi Camp (aka Mom) who listened and believed in me, my sister LeeAnne Beres and dad Doug Jackson who cheered me on, dear friend Carolyn Wence who radically shifted my direction, Greg Bell who was a generous expert and fueled my desire to write this book, and the amazing mentors who made a huge impact by teaching me life's biggest lessons through their leadership: Allan Mortenson, Sandra Peabody, Carol Clark Driskill, Cynthia Billette, Michael C. Smith, Sharyl Parker, and Sharon Lingenfelter... you all rock!

TABLE OF CONTENTS

3: ASSEMBLE YOUR TOOL KIT 31

Career Tools and Effective Job Searches

4: MISSION CONTROL, WE HAVE IGNITION 61

Launching your job search

5: Put on the Lights! It's Showtime! 121

Preparing for Interviews Impacts Your Career Direction

6: Time to Play Poker 165

*Playing to Win: How Negotiations Can Affect
Your Career Level and Pay For Years To Come*

PREFACE

Question: How have you arrived at your career destination?

Did you leave school and immediately land your dream job?

Are you even in the same field that you studied while in school?

...Or did you 'fall' into your line of work... through a series of circumstances?

When the American economy essentially tanked in 2007-2008, I noticed something. As wave after wave of layoffs, terminations, and closures hit companies across the country, clients from a wide array of industries arrived at my doorstep needing career help. I found them to be in a state of complete and utter shock. They had no idea the end was so near and had unexpectedly found themselves tossed out on the street, feeling completely betrayed by their former employers.

The secret that I found out: Most people have not actively managed or cultivated their careers as part of a conscious and well-thought-out long-term plan. In truth, most of us have ended up in our current jobs and/or careers as a result of a series of circumstances.

But what if there is a way to better control what circumstances happen... if we can purposefully network towards a career goal and positively influence our career outlook?

Many people caught up in the recent economic turmoil have worked in the same organization or industry for a long time (counting on retirement), or, through their networks, never had to look for a job before because the offers kept rolling in. It was an environment where people worked hard but bordered on complacency (versus advocacy) of themselves at the level needed to achieve career goals in today's employment environment.

Things have changed dramatically since the peak of yesterday's booming economy, and what worked back then for job searches simply is not viable now.

Today, dislocated or disenfranchised working professionals are facing significant challenges as they struggle to figure out how to find new jobs and to position themselves favorably to potential employers. But an even bigger obstacle in the way is the gaping void of knowledge on how to manage one's career which influences and impacts employer interest in their candidacy over similarly-qualified people competing for the same job.

As a result, many unemployed workers are not getting interview callbacks, while those who are unhappy in their current job are simply not advancing… or cannot find an escape.

These people have literally been "caught with their pants down" in their career because they haven't taken an active role in ensuring their employability.

Instead, they relied on a sense of job security and have coasted along, thinking that their employers would honor their dedication to the company or another company would notice how "awesome" they were… but then the economic meltdown occurred, and businesses started trimming payrolls and in some cases, closing their doors.

Suddenly, what employees previously regarded as job security evaporated the instant they were dismissed, and all of the countless hours (not to mention the "blood, sweat, and tears" that they had poured into the company as loyal employees) seemingly didn't matter anymore.

The word "loyalty" essentially died … it has become an out-of-circulation currency in an era where shorter-duration employees are always looking to jump to better opportunities and employers are actively trimming "dead wood" from staff teams in their quest for better efficiency and higher productivity.

Even now, as I continue to talk to clients, the new issue facing working professionals has become abundantly clear: most Americans have been incredibly naïve and complacent about managing their career outlook, and often don't even know what factors control their potential for advancement… let alone prepare themselves for looking for work should the unthinkable happen.

Complacency has no place in today's job market and business model. The concept of "top-grading" is becoming more and more commonplace as companies who have trimmed their staff down to a lean and mean core group are now evaluating how to best use the remaining staff to move the company forward.

Workers who thought they had bullet-proof company careers have suddenly found that gone, and are now left with dangling, unresolved questions:

"I did everything right, and was a top performer… How could this happen?"

"The boss and I were best pals… what went wrong?"

"Why me?"

But the truth is: **There is no such thing as job security anymore; it is now all about employability.**

And the biggest secret obstacle to your career rests on one thing and one thing only:

How complacent are you?

How are you managing your career outlook?

Are you awake or have you been asleep at the wheel?

Career management is a parallel universe co-existing alongside your actual career. It is everything you do from honing your personal value, developing your personal brand, to managing your career tools as well as launching a job search. In short, it exists and shadows every step of the way of your work life. However, most people have done nothing to jump into the driver's seat to take control of where they are going.

This book will help you understand the steps needed to achieve that objective. Being awake, aware, and proactive in managing your career outlook is your best insurance policy for being as employable as possible in the new era of career management.

This is an opportunity to wake up and drive your career... rather than letting it drive you.

WHY SHOULD I HIRE YOU?

ZEROING IN ON YOUR CAREER PURPOSE AND DEFINING YOUR VALUE PROPOSITION

**"If you really do put a small value upon yourself,
rest assured that the world will not raise your price."
- Anonymous**

One of the first and most critical steps of starting the career management process is for each of us to take ownership of why employers should consider hiring us.

In all likelihood, this is a reasonable interview question you might get thrown in your direction: "Why should we hire you?"

Most people have a tough time answering this question. The root cause? This could be one instance in which we really can blame our parents. From childhood, we've been taught not to boast, and our parents encouraged us to always be modest about our accomplishments lest we become braggarts.

The result?

Most of us are actually terrible at saying what exactly makes us good at what we do.

This is a good news/bad news scenario: the good news is that candidates applying for the same position aren't doing much better than you are in selling themselves. The bad news: you aren't doing much better!

To be successful in any aspect of managing our careers, we absolutely must take ownership of our successes and factor those wins into the bigger picture as to why someone would want to hire us.

There is a big difference between bragging and asserting your role in achieving positive things, and this chapter will explore how to gain a sense of how an employer (and you) should perceive your value.

PUMP YOURSELF UP

It is now necessary to view the employment marketplace as a competition with many contestants and incredibly high stakes. Winner takes all.

But in order to win, you must spotlight the benefits and value that makes you outshine your competition, with the goal to be chosen as the best candidate or to be considered for advancement/promotion.

But first, ask yourself this question: What is your value to employers?

Companies care about what you offer them – this is what keeps them engaged and interested throughout the application process, or when they are questioning who to retain and who to cut loose.

Can you answer this value question confidently and clearly, so they understand how what you offer benefits them?

From a company standpoint, if you can't tell someone why they should hire you in a value-oriented statement, how do you expect them to buy what you are selling as a potential new employee, or as someone they should keep on the payroll?

We all need to have a well-grounded approach on what our value is in the workplace, and how we can solve an employer's needs... whether we are looking for work or simply positioning ourselves for internal career advancement within an organization.

Being comfortable with owning your value and talking to others about it is the absolute lynchpin to having a purposeful career. You need to ASSERT yourself, which doesn't mean boasting... it means embracing what it is that you uniquely offer that would be of value to employers.

Remember, if you don't take ownership of your contributions and value, no one else will.

You and you alone are the driver of your own career destiny, no one else.

FOCUSING YOUR CAREER PURPOSE

Getting clarity of your career purpose will help you define your value proposition. However, many people struggle in this area because they aren't clear on their specific direction. This, in turn, impacts how they portray themselves and how they see their value.

Career purpose/direction can be determined by examining three different areas: job functions, career levels, and industry sectors. You will need to use these factors to zero in on connecting your background, skills, expertise, and experience to target positions.

Job functions are the core operational areas that every company has – like marketing, sales, accounting/finance, operations, administration, etc. They are the general departments that are specific to your particular field – and each field has unique considerations. Manufacturing might encompass inventory control, warehouse, shipping/receiving, production, and so forth.

Building a career direction means taking the job function and marrying it with the **career level**. That's the money part, which defines the salary you earn. Career levels are where you are on the proverbial organizational ladder: assistant, coordinator, manager, director, or president… you get the drift.

If you are in an industry-specific field, you can include the **industry sector** before the job function and career level to provide better targeting, but that is not necessary, especially if you are seeking to transfer your skills into a totally different sector.

The formula is as follows:

INDUSTRY + JOB FUNCTION + CAREER LEVEL = Career Target Direction

Figure 1: Example of job title headlines for building clarity in career direction

Industry	Function	Career Level
Hotel	Sales	Representative
Automotive	Marketing	Assistant
Manufacturing	Operations	Coordinator
Non-Profit	Development	Manager
IT	Product	Director
Association	Communications	Vice President

Each of these elements can be mixed and matched in order to connect the dots, and by going through this exercise, you are creating a clear characterization of yourself professionally. If you have a firm understanding of what your target career background entails, it will be a lot easier to communicate that to others when combined with your value proposition in that particular area.

DEFINING YOUR VALUE PROPOSITION

Companies see employees who demonstrate profitability or innovation as the most indispensible.

Knowing how you fit within the greater cogs of the company machine and the value of what you contribute to the overall organizational success is defined as your value proposition. It is also critical to understand that the value proposition has replaced the objective statement of the past. It is much more compelling to provide a reason to hire you instead of stating what you want out of the deal.

Defining this value proposition requires you to review what you excel in and create a short statement that clearly connects the benefits that you offer to your target audience in a way that appeals to their wants, needs, or values.

Simply put: Put on your "employer hat" and think about the pain-points an employer might have – if you were the boss and were hiring for this particular position, what would you want out of a candidate in terms of personal attributes and what they can deliver?

Knowing and feeling comfortable with your worth in terms of value to your current employer and prospective employers is a powerful tool in a job search. The proverbial "30-second commercial" or "elevator pitch" holds true today and needs to be integrated into every aspect of your job search arsenal.

Building your value proposition statement includes marrying the following elements into a statement that conveys your value.

Career Purpose + Top Accomplishments + Top Positive Attributes

REAL-WORLD EXAMPLE
High-energy senior marketing professional with 15+ years of experience in pioneering global award-winning corporate brand programs and communications that have led to $100 million increase in profits.

Tenacity in challenging status quo to discover breakthrough opportunities and define company through bold and memorable marketing campaigns.

By taking ownership of your best attributes that are of the most interest to employers, you can craft a compelling statement that connects your value to company needs. Embracing your value is the first step to career management because you understand the value of what you offer to employers... and that can set you apart from the competition.

Unleashing Your Personal Brand

Personal branding takes the value proposition and turns it into a short, pithy tagline which quickly and effectively establishes your personal brand to target audiences.

According to Dan Schawbel, author of *Me 2.0* and as one of the top personal branding gurus, advocates that all working professionals pay attention to the fact that **personal branding is critical to job search success.**

"Job seekers need to figure out how they want to position themselves in the crowded marketplace. In today's world, you need to become an expert at something and serve a particular industry or audience," Schawbel advises.

He also adds: "Job seekers need to develop a personal brand before other people do it for them. Hiring managers don't have much time to waste, so they need to know who you are and what you can do for them... it's your job to define that. It's also imperative that you build your personal brand online because the Internet is the global talent pool."

To work on your personal brand, take a sheet of paper and find a place where you won't be disturbed so you can concentrate. You'll need to do some deep soul-searching to find out the unique elements that you want to use in defining your career management strategy.

PERSONAL BRAND-BUILDING ACTIVITY:

- Brainstorm the things that get you fired up at work… what makes you passionate and excites you? Being centered on where the "fire" is in your belly will help you build an authentic brand that reflects the real you.
- Next, draw up a list of your personal attributes that you consider strengths, and brainstorm words that adequately describe what your work habits are in active terms.
- Research keywords commonly found in the types of jobs you are targeting or mirror your employment background.
- Start crafting a statement that conveys your value towards your career targets.

REAL-WORLD EXAMPLE:

A client of mine was struggling with her personal brand as a corporate communications manager. Her job tasks included sending out company information through multiple channels to a large number of employees spread across multiple units. But through all the competing messages, she was able to create frequently read publications that were useful employee communication tools.

Her personal brand: **"Adding Volume to the Corporate Voice."** Short, succinct, and impactful.

Weaving in personal traits, specialties, and interests can create a personal brand that cleverly portrays yourself in a unique light.

Another client of mine looked like a job-hopper as she changed employers every 1-2 years. As it turns, she actually was a high-powered sales person who was actively recruited by start-up companies to generate a high volume of initial revenue, and once that was achieved, her work was done. We solved the problem posed by frequent job changes by billing her as: "Delivering Quick Revenue Infusions for Start-Ups," which better positioned her expertise.

Take the time to get this brand down on paper; you will be able to build value into not just your résumé, but also into your psyche so your worth to potential employers is deeper under your skin.

Being connected to your self-worth can literally make the difference between being offered the job or not.

But also be aware that refining and tweaking this personal branding statement is a continuous process, and can and likely will also change over time as you grow professionally and expand your career reach.

Once developed, you can find many different applications for your elevator pitch. Use it in job interviews. Post it on your LinkedIn profile. Tweet it. Include it on your website and use this as a basis to write a cover letter. The key is to COMPEL people to want to get to know you or hire you, and as every advertiser would affirm: You need to show the audience what's in it for them. And the best way to get to that point is to understand what you have to offer and how it stands out above the other competing options.

Taking this strategy will give you power and purpose in your job search and also provide a clear path on how you define yourself within a work environment. How you positively project and perceive yourself makes a big impact on how others see you as well.

It's also important to maintain consistency for your brand across all channels. If you have different messages and brands, it comes across as disconnected and incongruous to prospective employers. The same holds true for the photo that you use to associate with yourself. Going to sites like Gravatar are great ways to establish a consistent online visual identity for yourself that is ported over to many websites when you comment on articles or post updates... essentially following you across those different platforms.

The key is that once you define your personal brand, make it consistent across all communication channels. Having multiple personas confuses audiences and doesn't help reinforce your message.

We'll explore how to cultivate a reliable and consistent representation in all career channels in Chapter 3.

2

Putting Your Game Face On

Proactively Managing Your Career Building Blocks: Your Reputation

"The key to change... is to let go of fear."
- Rosanne Cash

Establishing yourself in the workplace or beginning the hunt for a new job is probably one of the scariest things you can ever do. Most people express a great deal of fear when faced with new opportunities.

But it can also be one of the most powerful and rewarding experiences. We grow the most when we overcome things that we fear, and can learn new things about ourselves that can add dimension and depth to our character as well as our understanding of the world.

Someone once told me that change is the most terrifying when we actually desire or need it the most. This, in turn, can make us feel like we are standing on the edge of a precipice; uncertain as to whether we can make that leap of faith or not.

Understanding the building blocks of your career management strategy will help you become a smarter and wiser job seeker, and ultimately help you overcome the very fears that could be holding you back from making that leap.

Fear is real. And what we are really scared of is the failure of our actions. Life's lessons will tell you that there never is a guarantee for success in any decision you make. It always comes down to a series of calculated risks and educated guesses... nothing more and nothing less. Sometimes you win, and sometimes you lose. It's the risk we take, and the fear comes from the uncertainty from the lack of any kind of guarantee.

This chapter will help you work through the core elements of building your career so you can consciously have a good measure of your value in the workplace and yet be ready for opportunities that come along... or be adequately prepared to respond if the unimaginable happens, and conquer those fears.

NEW GRADUATES

New graduates starting out in their careers are facing one of the toughest job markets in history. What few jobs that are open have literally hundreds of applicants, some of whom are vastly overqualified, putting newly minted workers at a marked disadvantage.

One of the biggest problems grads face are their credentials and how they prepare to build their career. While most career centers try to provide counseling to students on how to bridge their background that translates to the work world, many students aren't listening or aren't given any reasons for the strategy behind the document or a focused job search.

Here are some tips that you'll not likely be taught in school.

- **Your reputation is now on a piece of paper.**
In school, you are known for what you wear and who you hang around with, and you've pretty much been with the same age group for your entire life. Now, everything you are all about goes on your résumé (a piece of paper) – where you worked, what you did, and how you did it: this is now the reputation that will follow you throughout your entire career. This is a HUGE shift in thinking.

- **Be patient and you will be rewarded.**
Understand that in your job search or during your career, things aren't going to move as fast as you like. You want it now, but then so does everyone else. If you can learn patience, you will be rewarded, and even recognized for having the maturity to find the right opportunity, versus trying to force it.

- **Your career will be a *series* of choices, not *"a"* choice.**
The average high school student is going to have an average of 10.8 jobs in their lifetime… so you definitely won't be putting all your eggs in one basket. What you do for a living is going to change… many times. Think of it as a constant evolution process.

- **Tread lightly and carefully.**
The office political environment can play out in a similar fashion to social cliques back in school… with deadlier consequences. Gossip never has a place in the workplace, but it does happen, and that person you confided in could just as easily turn around and stab you in the back… torpedoing your career. Instead, keep your own counsel and zip your lips!

- **Don't leave your dirty dishes in the office sink... your office mates are not your mom.**

Everything you do from this point forward is business, and not bound by any bonds other than your employment agreement. It's pretty darned scary to be suddenly put out in the cold after having warm, supportive environments at home and school. You will now be judged by your actions and should always do the right thing whether you think someone is watching or not... and never expect someone to be there to catch you when you fall. That's called life, and over the course of your career, you are going to make mistakes and have to learn from them. That's called experience.

CAREER CHANGERS

Some professionals are rethinking their career choices due to the continued economic instability plaguing America. Perhaps they lost their job through cutbacks or layoffs, but instead of viewing this critical juncture as being the end of the world, perhaps this is an opportunity to spark a reinvention of themselves.

This can also be true for others who are yearning for greener pastures to find meaning in their work. Many baby boomers have become interested in an encore career that repackages their existing skill sets into an entirely different career field that aligns more closely with their interests or values.

However, finding that connection between vocation (the work you have to do to get paid) and the avocation (the work you'd like to do) doesn't necessarily match up perfectly skill-wise.

So how does one leap-frog from one career field to another, if they aren't related? Even more importantly, how do you start to rebuild your career all over again from scratch?

REAL-WORLD EXAMPLE

One of my favorite examples of this conundrum was a client who has been a writer, but had a passion for wine. She had taken a staggering number of enology (wine) classes on her own, and had even visited Napa and Sonoma Valley wineries to participate in the harvest and spend time with wine-makers on her own dime.

Her goal: to be a wine marketing representative. We paired her experience with writing marketing materials and conducting sales activities associated with that work with her intensive wine knowledge. The end product? We wrote a functional résumé, blending those skill sets together, and presto! A new wine marketing consultant was born!

But how would you make this work for yourself?

The following areas can be keys to bridging that gap with connecting activities in order to transition from your current career area to the type of work that you'd rather be doing:

- **Volunteering.**

Most busy professionals have some kind of volunteer activity going on in their lives, but in addition to "giving back," volunteering is also a great conduit to finding out whether a specific industry is really a fit for you. And if you are seeking a career in this area, volunteering can provide skills, background, and contacts, as well as make you become a "known" quantity to a particular organization. You never know where this might take you, and is a positive avenue that gives back to an organization while at the same time allowing for safe career exploration.

- **Involvement/memberships.**

Practically every industry has some type of professional trade or membership association. These organizations are troves of information and, more importantly, contacts. By targeting an industry sector, you can

15

research the professional groups associated with that area, and then do some digging. What kind of networking and educational activities does each group offer? Focus in on one or two groups, then get involved as a member and build industry credibility, attend networking events, and gain additional sector-specific knowledge through educational programs. This can do wonders for your portfolio and contact network!

- **Education.**

Formal training and professional development are also excellent ways to build up skills and expertise in a new career field. Credit can be given for professional experience already gained in a field, so starting from scratch often isn't necessary. Many institutions and certifying agencies not only provide the "classroom" portion of learning, but also have connecting activities through outplacement or internships that enable practical, real-world experience. Marrying your current relevant skill sets with formal education can help you shift career direction significantly in ways that you've never dreamed!

- **Vocational immersion.**

An exciting new concept for new career-field seekers is to immerse oneself into a particular career area without jumping ship from a current job. "Test driving" one's dream job is the idea behind Vocation Vacations, an organization founded by visionary leader Brian Kurth that allows people to explore new career directions within a safe environment. "Vocationers" are paired up with industry experts as mentors, and spend a pre-determined amount of time (akin to a vacation period) with that mentor, and learn the "inside scoop" and ropes of that particular business. Tapping into an expert's knowledge can help you determine if this is the right fit before you make any significant life and career-altering decisions.

RE-ENTERING THE WORKFORCE

Life happens. Sometimes, we simply can't predict the types of things that can waylay the best of intentions and plans. What we had hoped to achieve or accomplish within a set period of time simply doesn't happen because other things come up that we have no control over... and those things suddenly take precedence over everything else.

And that's okay.

When it comes to your career (and life in general), the thing you always must always remember is that we are all doing the best we can under the circumstances, and trying to make the best decisions possible with the information we have at the time.

Sometimes, when we look to the past, we clearly see mistakes that we made and now wish that we had chosen differently. Or, we might realize that we did what we wanted and/or needed to, but those previous choices now make our current situation much more challenging.

This could be the situation that you are facing right now... have you been out of work for awhile? Maybe you took time off to raise a family or take care of an ailing parent. Or maybe you tried another career field and it didn't quite turn out as you had anticipated, so you are now coming back to something that you are better at and love. Or, perhaps, you took time away from the work world to fulfill other personal goals, such as finishing up college or taking a soul-searching trip around the world to learn about yourself or other cultures.

The hardest challenge is, as most people find out, how to account for that time away from the workforce.

Rebuilding one's career can take some time, and here are some tips that can help you get back into the swing of things by minimizing your career liabilities.

- **Refer to your time away as "Personal sabbatical" or "Professional sabbatical."**
Take ownership of your time out of the workforce and sift through what the positive and relevant highlights that came out of that time. By running away and trying to hide it, you are tearing yourself down instead of building yourself up.

- **Brush up on your skills.**
If you have not been working for several years, you might consider taking a class to brush up on your skills or address any skill gaps that could be potential obstacles to your employment. A minor investment on your end could mean a big pay-off in the future by making your background more attractive to employers.

- **Volunteer.**
Volunteering in your target field on a regular basis where you have ownership of projects and leadership is a great way to rebuild your career direction. Put your skills, knowledge, and expertise into action.

- **Network like there's no tomorrow.**
Chances are that during your time out of the workforce, you have gravitated away from your specific career field in pursuit of other activities or interests, and your network has suffered as a result.

Now is the time to throw yourself out there and network with a vengeance. Reconnect to existing contacts and join industry organizations to meet new people. With somewhere between 80-90% of jobs being found through someone you know, sitting at home clicking "send" on your computer simply isn't going to get you anywhere. You need to be out there meeting people.

- **Connect to industry thought leaders.**

Follow them on social media channels and if they are based locally, see if you can set up time for coffee. You need to learn anything and everything you can about industry changes and emerging trends, and these people are powerful influencers. Who knows? They also might be motivated to help you in your job search. But you won't know unless you connect with them.

- **Ask for help.**

There is no shame in asking for help. Review your contact lists and don't be shy about reaching out to them and asking for help in being introduced to people in your target field if there is a connection.

Following these tips to address long gaps in employment history caused by personal circumstances will help you make yourself more interesting to employers. Your career depends on it!

All of these options are viable ways to gain inside knowledge, understanding, and expertise to take that "leap" into a new career field. The best part is that you can engage in these activities while at the same time maintaining your current employment until you feel that you are ready to transition to your avocation. It's exciting and invigorating, and can open up brand new avenues as well as bring new meaning and purpose to your work life!

BUILDING VALUE IN AN ORGANIZATION

Proactive career management means that you actively create and cultivate personal value within an organization.

This means taking a closer look at what are you currently doing, and developing strategies to make yourself more indispensable and more valuable.

Bring value to an organization by carefully making sure you meet all the goals set for your on-the-job performance. Even creating an annual checklist to follow on a daily basis can help you meet those goals if you are struggling with achieving basic expectations.

You should also step up to take on additional responsibility whenever possible, but be careful about not becoming a "dumping" ground for undesired projects from co-workers anxious to rid themselves of a distasteful project. By shouldering additional tasks, this can become an opportunity to expand your on-the-job knowledge and also develop new, transferrable skills while building your value within an organization and demonstrating initiative.

Another thing you can do is identify conferences, workshops, or other forms of professional development that can enhance your job-specific knowledge. If there is an opportunity to act as a "train-the-trainer" or add to the overall company knowledge base, you also become known as a subject matter expert. Employers rely on these specialists as core contributors and by acting like one, this enhances your organizational value.

Additionally, if your company has any kind of internal committees or task forces, be assertive and volunteer to participate, which will boost your leadership quotient. An added benefit is that this is a way to stay in the limelight with company managers.

Which leads to another important component of career management: You absolutely must communicate your wins which can and will make a difference in how people perceive you. This does not mean crowing about it in an egotistical way... it means simply that you need to proactively and deliberately let supervisors and other stakeholders know about your successes, whether you directly achieved them or were part of a team that did.

REAL-WORLD EXAMPLE

One of my clients purposefully provided very detailed staff reports about their project successes and inroads to the department director, who reported these to the board. Over time, this person earned a stellar reputation within the organization as a strategic thinker which led to significant career advancement into higher leadership levels. It was a slow, methodical process, but being aware of how each piece of the daily puzzle fits into the bigger career picture is what everyone should be thinking about for long-term career building.

See Figure 3 for ways to get the message out about your achievements. Stating the facts about what you've done and relating them back to organizational goald is a very smart way to manage perceptions of your value internally.

Figure 3: Get the message out: If you don't tell them... they won't know.

Communicating your value within an organization doesn't mean getting a bullhorn to shout out to the rafters how awesome you are. But you can't ever assume that the organizational leaders are immediately in touch with what your value has been to the organization.

Instead, it much more of a long-term, measured approach. Here are some ways to keep your successes top-of-mind to supervisors and bosses so you cultivate a reputation of being a positive contributor:

- Weekly staff reports
- End of year summaries
- Direct emails to boss about specific wins
- Ask happy customers to put satisfaction in writing
- Provide regular project updates
- Put metrics into place if there aren't any to measure progress
- Proactively anticipate supervisor informational needs

Remember: supervisors and bosses won't automatically know, so now is the time to proactively create your own internal marketing campaign to build personal brand awareness.

BUILDING EXTERNAL VALUE

The same concepts used in building other people's perception of the value that you offer internally also apply for external value, but it actually unfolds in two different contexts.

Building external value can take the form of building the company's external value through you (by virtue of your actions and personal integrity), while having the effect of boosting your own reputation at the same time.

REAL-WORLD EXAMPLE

Marge worked at a tourism bureau where her job was to promote the area as a destination to sightseeing groups from all over the world. She could have just stuck with doing exactly that, but instead, took it one step further. Thinking beyond herself and her company, Marge realized that most tourists weren't coming to visit her city; they often visited other areas of the state too. She started contacting surrounding tourist bureaus to let them know that the groups were coming into town, so those tourism organizations could also market to them. By giving these bureaus outside her immediate area some much-needed leads, Marge not only helped the clients who wanted to get information from these destinations, but she also made her own company look good by sharing information.

It became a win-win situation where clients got the information that they needed, other tourist bureaus got qualified leads, and Marge's organization earned goodwill within the hospitality industry by being a generous sharer of sales leads.

But another thing happened that was a windfall Marge had not expected: By acting in this capacity, she was also building up her reputation within the industry as a valuable partner who was committed to the bigger picture... and helping others.

Like Marge, the positive side effect of building up organizational value externally is that you also benefit by cultivating a positive image and reputation of your leadership. But you need to be careful to not make this the sole motivating factor... you must always be authentic in your desire to put the organization or industry first; the rest will follow as your own reputation enhancement.

SOCIAL MEDIA AUDIT

Your reputation is your career lifeblood. If it becomes tainted, your career could die. And that includes what is said about you online.

With so many social media platforms out there, it is more important than ever to carefully manage what you say and how you say it online.

The sad thing is that there still are an awful lot of people out there who are ignorant to the fact that their tweets or posts become part of their online digital diary, recorded forever for posterity.

With 4 out of 5 employers using social media to learn more about prospective candidates for jobs, the online representations of these people could prove to be not exactly what that company had in mind... based on the applicant's opinions as expressed in what they feel is personal cyberspace.

Others blatantly don't care about what potential employers might perceive or think about them. Damn the torpedoes, they say. "I am who I am, and I won't apologize for it."

These people are opinionated as part of their personal brand, and that very reason is what attracts people to them – these people are the ones who will say what they think. It's a breath of fresh air in a sea of vanilla people afraid to "rock the boat." But when it comes down to looking for work, either employers are interested in this uniqueness, or else end up being extremely repelled. By taking this attitude, you do put your employability at risk by alienating those who do not agree with you.

Conversely, other people completely resist being online, citing legitimate privacy concerns or a general disdain for any online networks. The problem is that with so many employers rushing in to embrace technology, these technophobes are endangering themselves further… essentially, if they aren't on the Internet, they are invisible. Having no information can be seen as a complete career liability. Some employers might interpret these folks as having nothing to contribute or else are so far behind the times that they are now obsolete.

Before proactively launching a personal online branding initiative, the best place to start is by conducting a social media audit to find out exactly what already exists online about you.

The easiest method to this is to simply "Google" yourself to see how you appear in search results. What comes up when you do a search on your name? Is the information positive? Are the first results about you? Does your name even show up?

There are countless other measurement tools online that can provide insights on how you appear (or not), depending on your level of technological sophistication. Common ones include Klout, Google Analytics, PeerIndex, Addictomatic, Grader.com, and various insight tools that measure social networking sites such as Facebook, Foursquare, Flickr, and Twitter. Additionally, as technology keeps evolving, new tools debut every day, so stay abreast of some of these trends by following great technology resources like Mashable.com to learn about ones which are the most useful.

Depending on what you see in those results, you'll have a better idea of where you should concentrate your online brand development efforts.

BUILDING POSITIVE CONTENT

If you are new to getting yourself online, or haven't touched your social media profiles for awhile, this is a good time to start building new content about yourself. Figure 4 provides some great ways to get out there.

Proactive career managers create positive content that gets them onto employer radar screens. Try building content using these tools (new ones are coming along every day).

Figure 3:

Blogs	Writing industry articles	Own websiteç
LinkedIn profile	Belonging to industry	Social bookmarking
Facebook page	groups/associations	About.me
Twitter account	YouTube channel	Discussion
Google+ profile	BeKnown	groups/forums
Positive comments	Vizibility	Writing e-book/book
on other blogs	BranchOut	
Getting listed in online	ZoomInfo	
directories	Plaxo	

Don't feel like you need to try and get set up on all of these sites immediately – in truth, an effective approach is the "advance then retreat, then advance again" strategy where you don't try to undertake learning each individual site all in one sitting. So much information requires experimentation, adjustment, and digestion before you can move on into the finer details of what each platform offers and how you might use it.

In all likelihood, you won't learn an entire social site in one sitting, so it will require you to explore, set up the basics, then step away for a little while to absorb what you just learned, then go back a little later. Bit by bit, you'll grow your knowledge and understanding of each of these platforms and better understand how they fit best in your positive online content-building strategies. Also be aware of new and emerging platforms... embrace them and see how effective they are as you explore their features.

ADDRESSING NEGATIVE CONTENT

Unfortunately, there are situations where someone who bears a grudge takes to the airwaves (or in this case, the Internet) to gripe about you publicly and attempt to tear you down. These people ("trolls") are judgmental and generally unpleasant... usually the result of having personal issues or being disgruntled due to some kind of perceived slight.

Unfortunately, when an employer does a Google search on you and finds these negative comments in search results, you aren't present in the room with them to try and explain the situation.

So what can you do to bury this "digital dirt?" It hurts having negative information out there that can sully your reputation and your personal brand. But there are some steps you can take to address it.

- **Clean up online information that you can control.**

If it is your profile that is revealing unsavory details or content, then evaluate it thoroughly and remove all negative references. However, it make take a little time before the new profile information re-populates web servers, so the old information may stick around for a little while. Additionally, be conscious about what you say online – negative or critical comments could be accurate, but could end up reflecting badly upon you if the bad outweighs the good.

- **Request information be taken down.**

If someone has posted something bad about you, one option might be to contact them directly to address their concerns and then request they remove that reference. It is a long shot, but could help you remove a potential liability posted online for everyone to see. If you are having trouble identifying the site owner, try looking them up on the WhoIs domain registry.

- **Set up Google alerts.**

Whatever is posted online about you can and will change… content is constantly added, so use Google alerts to get notifications about any new online references. It can help you immediately jump on new posts or content that could be a liability.

- **Provide online rebuttals addressing negative content.**

A carefully crafted response to negative posts or comments about you can help deflate the writer's assertions. But be careful about coming across as defensive, which could backfire and cause further damage.

- **Report the problem to Google.**

You can report any content to this site that you believe warrants removal based on applicable laws, and they will take the site out of search results.

- **Report abuse.**

If someone has a vendetta and makes inappropriate posts about you, you can complain to moderators or the sponsoring organizations and report the person's comments as abuse.

- **Hire legal counsel.**

Lawyers can create cease-and-desist letters that have more teeth than any email you could send, and can be a basis for prosecuting someone for libel or defamation if their malicious words are shared with someone other than you.

- **Bury it.**

Concentrate your energy and resources by generating so much positive content (see previous section) that any "bad" results get pushed down to page 3 of any Google results.

Jacob Share, founder of JobMob and author of the *Ultimate Twitter Job Search Guide*, wrote a brilliant blog post, "200+ Resources and Tips To Help Manage Your Reputation Online" which can be found at: http:// bit.ly/QhLD and is one of the best tools for managing your reputation.

Using tools included on Share's list enables you to engage in active career management by containing negative content and minimizing it through pro-active generation of positive data to cultivate a favorable online presence.

KEEPING UP APPEARANCES: CONSISTENCY MATTERS

Transitioning from the online world to real life, cultivating a positive brand for your personal appearance is equally important.

Remember the good old days of high school? How what you wore defined your image?

Surprise. The work world isn't much different. The only thing that has changed is that for the most part, no one is going to say anything directly to you about what you wear... they simply won't hire or promote you if the image that you project doesn't fit within the company culture.

What we wear and our appearance DOES impact our career... from the first few seconds in an interview to what you choose from your closet on a daily basis.

Sound trivial? It is, but as the employer sees it: it isn't.

How you represent yourself is also how the company you work for represents itself to its customers, both internally and externally.

REAL-WORLD EXAMPLE

Way back (I won't say how long ago)... in my first job, on the very first day, I was pulled aside by my supervisor who said she was going to have to send me home to change my clothing.

Flabbergasted and completely humiliated, I asked why. She smiled, and in a very kind, sympathetic voice, told me to look around the corporate environment and see what others are wearing.

Suddenly, my eyes were opened and I saw people wearing suits and other formal business attire. Then I looked down at myself... I was a college student (and at the time, leggings and big shirts were "in"), and immediately realized what she was saying. Ironically, in the college environment, what I was wearing was generally considered somewhat "dressy" compared to the usual fare of sweatshirts and sweatpants common on campus. In fact, some of my friends had even commented how nice I looked, and I had proudly replied that I was going to my first day on the job.

Oooh... was that first day ever a learning experience.

The rule of thumb is that you if you don't take your personal image seriously, then how can anyone else?

You should always dress one level ABOVE your current position. Obviously, you don't want to overdo it, and in many companies, particularly on the West Coast, office attire has been slipping into "business casual," which is a far cry from the stuffy 3-piece suit days.

But you are what you wear, and if you demonstrate care and cultivation of your personal image, others will pick up on this and this perception will shape their view of you.

Be strategic about what you buy; don't always go for the cheapest price because sometimes, the poor tailoring can become readily apparent after wearing the outfit even once. Be willing to make an investment into finer materials that aren't too trendy so you can extend the clothing's lifetime.

The point is: investing in your wardrobe is really investing in yourself and your personal brand. Cultivating your personal brand appearance can have positive, far-reaching impacts on your career and future advancement.

3

ASSEMBLE YOUR TOOL KIT

CAREER TOOLS AND
EFFECTIVE JOB SEARCHES

"It's so much easier to write a résumé than to craft a spirit."
- Anna Quindlen

But in all fairness, writing a résumé is no easy task, especially when you are trying to communicate the spirit of the person behind it.

Think about this: when was the last time that you purposefully updated this document versus scrambling at the last minute? The majority of people wait until they absolutely HAVE TO and find it a horrible, painful process. As a result, the résumé is one of the most commonly neglected items in your career tool kit (and possibly the most hated, too!).

To do it right, creating or updating a résumé requires a great deal of attention and effort to accurately put your best foot forward.

People who are in active career management mode don't delay updating this important career asset. They see the résumé as a dynamic, vibrant, and more importantly, a *living* career document.

Understanding what your tools are, including résumés, is an important part of managing your career. Now that you have developed your career purpose, value proposition, personal brand, and started cultivating a positive professional reputation, it's time to look at the different career management devices you need to use in order to be successful.

RÉSUMÉS

Are you ready?

Okay, here it is: 80% of all the résumés out there suck. And in an informal survey I've been conducting with HR and recruiting professionals, this is a relatively conservative number, so yes, I mean that they really suck. As in spelling/grammar/usage/punctuation errors, ugly or non-existent formatting, lack of keywords, cutting and pasting job duties instead of listing valuable contributions, inclusion of photos and other non-relevant personal information, and the ever-so-outdated objective statement which is the constant thorn in the side of anyone who reads the document, just to name a few.

These horrible elements are still out there and circulating in all of their hideous, error-ridden, and totally ineffective glory.

There's a reason why so many résumé writers, human resource managers, and career professionals are constantly tweeting and writing articles on this subject. We are literally screaming at the top of lungs... job seekers simply *have* to punch it up a notch in today's highly sophisticated job market.

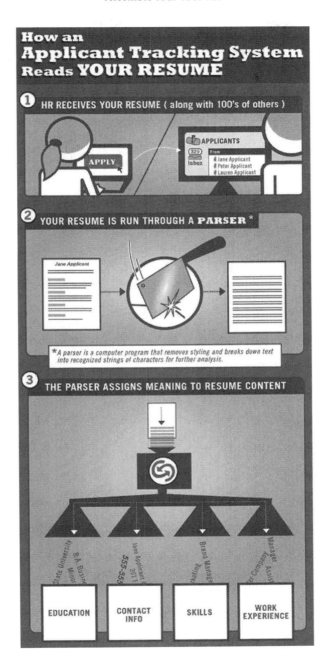

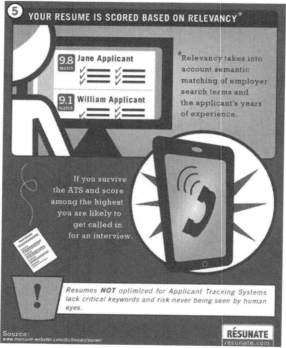

Credit: Resunate™, Professional Diversity Network

But the problem is that there are a lot of people, to their own detriment, who simply are not "getting" it. Whether they are just plain ignorant or too egotistical to admit their résumé isn't up to current snuff.

You absolutely need to elevate your résumé to the next level whether you buy a how-to book to do it yourself, or hire a professional. It's a challenging task, and unfortunately, there is no standardized format which makes creating this document a huge challenge to people who only tackle it once in a blue moon.

Another significant challenge about résumé writing is that employers are discriminating against job seekers. They won't admit it; it is obviously illegal and extremely difficult to prove, but happens all the time… The goal of writing this document is to write to the audience while not tipping your hand by giving an employer any personal information that could lead to any potential bias.

Add in the reality that many companies use Applicant Tracking Systems (ATS) to scan résumés for matching keywords that match job announcements, and this is becoming an even tougher task facing unwitting job seekers who struggle for hours on their résumé document and don't even know about this software.

The purpose of this section is _not_ to provide you with detailed step-by-step instruction on how to write a résumé (please read Britton Whitcomb's book) but you should be aware of the key things that have changed about résumé development that you need to know.

- **Email addresses can hurt.**
Eliminate references in your email address that are related to age, politics, personal preferences, health conditions, or any other kind of activism that could put your candidacy at risk if the intended

audience has concerns or biases against those areas. What do you think "Gnarly1941@emailaddress.com" might convey? Or MaryJaneReefer@ emailaddress.net?" A surprising number of people continue to send out résumés that continue to have what I call "goofy" email addresses. Safest bet? Your name. Your name as the email address is your best bet. If you have a common name, then add some random number or variation that still makes it clear that this is your name, but don't use your birth or graduation date, let alone your age in those numeric representations. And also don't use your employer's address either... you don't want to give off the wrong signal to potential employers that you are willing to abuse work resources for a personal job search.

- **Ditch the objective statement.**

Employers don't care what you want... which is what an objective is all about. Objective statements are *so* 1970s... get rid of it. The person considering hiring you has only one thing on their mind: what are you going to do for *them*?

Remember how the career purpose was discussed earlier in this book? Use your new job title headline as the lynchpin of the entire document – the title should be the same as or similar to your target job position while at the same time serving to "theme" your document. This will help you stay focused in developing your résumé while at the same time, giving the employer only what they want to know.

Then, include your value proposition right below your job title headline to provide the case as to why an employer should hire you. After all, of all times in the entire job search process, telling an employer why you are the best candidate and why you stand out should take place in the résumé, wouldn't you agree?

- **Include keywords.**

Figure 2: Quantifying Work Results

Employers want to see value. Bosses are squeezing out every penny that they can just to keep departments and companies afloat. It's almost like the words 'return on investment' are practically carved above the doorway over the office entrance.

Keep track of your accomplishments and results.

Here are some tools to get you thinking more critically about your own recordkeeping:

- Performance appraisals/reviews
- Professional development (conferences, conventions, etc. attended)
- Plan of Work
- Checklists
- Staff reports
- Client, supervisor or colleague kudos
- Internal productivity reports
- Awards or other industry/company recognition or honors
- Any new systems/procedures/initiatives/projects/products
- Published/Quoted/Featured
- Patents or other work-related accomplishments
- Industry certifications
- Attendance
- Positions of leadership in relevant industry organizations
- Annual company report/success metrics
- Superlatives – like the "biggest sale in company history"

If you don't state it, they don't know you can do it. Plus, factoring in how Applicant Tracking Systems (ATS) read your career document, you need to get the right cloud of critical "keywords" that are actually the skills required to do the job. A great resource is www.onetonline.org to get some keywords, but be sure to read multiple job announcements (whether you plan on applying for them or not) to develop a general list of the top keywords, then include them in a brief section on your résumé called "Career Expertise" – that sounds a lot smarter than "Skills List" or "Qualifications."

- **Don't stick your awards/accolades at the bottom of your résumé.**

Most people don't know what to do with mentions of industry awards or recognition, so invariably, they go right to the very end of the résumé… which is exactly the least-read part of the entire document.

Create a separate section called "Notable Achievements" that comes after your skill sets and before your work history to fall within the most-read critical 1/3 of the first page of your document. Remember… the cream rises to the top, so get those industry distinctions up where employers can see them and see how awesome you are!

Include things like your awards (industry, peer, supervisor, etc), patents, publications, sessions that you have presented as a speaker, and any relevant industry certifications to make sure you stand out. Do NOT include references to financial incentives that you won; employers don't care about that so keep that information out.

- **Quantify results.**

This is a wake-up call for each and every one of us: **The very principles of benchmarking company results/performance are the same ones that every working professional should apply towards their own career management.**

When it comes down to trimming staff levels, who do you think a business might keep: The employee who just trundled along, day by day, or the one who kept a dynamic record of their positive contributions to the company?

Most people don't do a good job in this area, so if this is a problem for you, the good news is that you aren't alone.

But showing your value to your current employer or using your value proposition to find a new position with another company will require you to transfer company benchmarking and performance to goal into strategic career management... by showing results.

The results that matter, however, vary by industry.

For-profit companies generally only care about whether you make money, save money, or save time.

Non-profit organizations want to know how you have reached more stakeholders, built more sponsorship support, or raised awareness within new groups.

For people working in schools and educational institutions, ask yourself: how have you increased test scores and boosted learning?

If you work at a governmental agency, think about how you have boosted efficiencies, program reach, or compliance levels.

So, instead of copying and pasting your job duties from a position description, you'll need to create value-driven statements that quantify your results and answers the employer's question of "So what?" which will persuade them to hire you.

REAL-WORLD EXAMPLE

"Delivered 150% revenue increase over previous year by developing new product which met previously unmet customer need for irrigation equipment."

This value-driven example sounds a lot better than a job description task such as "Monitor client feedback to identify potential new product ideas."

- **Include "Professional Development" as a sub-header under your EDUCATION section.**

This sounds much more polished than "training" and conveys a different level of how you feel about your résumé document. You ABSOLUTELY must keep adding to this section of your résumé, and this symbolizes one of the three major career elements driving your career – right here in your document.

Look at what classes, workshops, training, conferences, conventions, seminars, industry certification, webinars, etc. that you have taken and how long ago they took place.

This is the moment where you can suddenly start looking at your résumé as a dynamic career road map – **it isn't a stagnant obituary listing your career background!!!**

People who are actively managing their careers see this section as a road map that can point out growth opportunities or use this to identify career weaknesses that they need to spend some time and energy shoring up.

Ask yourself the following questions about your professional development background:

Where are your skill gaps?

Where are the areas where you need to update your knowledge?

How can you gain access to cutting-edge information/trends to put you on the forefront of your industry?

What knowledge would you and your career benefit from adding?

What skill sets would be of value to your employer or future employers?

What kinds of professional development programs are leaders in your industry participating in that enhances their own job expertise or industry knowledge?

When was the last time you took a class?

If your last professional development class took place a long time ago, you could be perceived as being behind the times. Demonstrating that you are up to speed and current with emerging trends and technology can help stand out from other candidates; otherwise, you could be left behind.

Remember: The early adopters of today are the influencers of tomorrow.

Another important point to understand is that by keeping a current (within last 5-7 years) list of your professional development activities, you are also communicating to employers that you possess a thirst for knowledge and learning. This is a great way to show that you care about doing a good job, which is a powerful and assertive subliminal message to send to prospective employers.

One last point about the EDUCATION section on your résumé: Unless you are in an educational field or highly scientific industry, it is not necessary to include your graduation date(s).

Including this information actually could end up being a liability for new entrants to the workforce as well as more mature workers – discrimination based on age happens on both ends of the spectrum, and listing graduation dates is a dead-giveaway in general as employers can do the math.

You also do not need to include your G.P.A. or that you were on the "Academic All-Star Cheerleading Team" – it is a sad-yet-true sign of the times that employers usually only care about one thing when it comes to educational background – did you graduate? Yes or no? Then they move on, so don't use a lot of résumé space providing information that really isn't critical to your candidacy.

- **Affiliations/Involvement.**

Affiliations are what you belong to (like memberships and groups) and involvement is where you volunteer or contribute as a leader. Just like professional development, these are career management drivers.

Put yourself in this scenario: If you are the employer, and you have two candidates who are equally qualified up to this point, and one person has a robust section detailing their involvement and leadership while the other does not, who do you think they will select?

The secret to creating an AFFILIATIONS/INVOLVEMENT section on your résumé is that it communicates one thing: You have <u>initiative</u>.

Employers like people who don't just move papers around their desk and do only the minimum requested... they want dynamic, go-getters

42

who don't let moss grow. By being engaged in your industry, having a robust network, and being a generous expert who gives back, you are establishing your own subject matter knowledge and leadership which, in turn, becomes highly attractive to employers.

This also means you are driven to improve yourself and do a better job, while positively impacting those around you.

From a career management standpoint, showing involvement and engagement in your target field is a powerful tool to persuade an employer to hire you.

- **Name your résumé document.**
A typical mistake we all make… being in a hurry and have a working document titled "résumé." It gets tweaked then saved, and we hit "send." But what happens when the employer receiving your document gets dozens of other résumés from other applicants… with the exact same document title? It gets pretty confusing really fast.

In summary: You have done nothing to distinguish yourself from the other applicants, and need to rethink this approach.

Part of developing career branding for yourself is thinking exhaustively about every facet of how you are represented. The easiest solution with the document name situation? Use your name, as in "Jane_Doe_Product_Manager_Resume.doc" which helps the employer keep tabs and also track the position if there are concurrent openings for different jobs.

BIZARRO (NEW) © 2011 DAN PIRARO.
KING FEATURES SYNDICATE

- **Proofread your document for errors.**
Read your résumé at least 4 times, then have at least two others proof it as well. Don't count on spell check to catch all of your errors. Some of the most common problems include capitalization, punctuation, improper use, grammar, and spelling. Many professional résumé writers use this trick to catch problems: they start proofing the document from the bottom up. That helps the brain to not "gloss" over sentences because you are making yourself think differently by reading everything in reverse.

- **"Massaging" previous job titles and dates can be hazardous to your career health.**
One particularly startling fact keeps rearing its ugly head when client résumés hit my inbox: People take exceptional liberties regarding previous job titles they've held when listing them on their résumé.

Uh Oh. Cue the "Dum… da dum dum" music.

Are you feeling remotely uncomfortable yet?

Most human resource and hiring managers see "Job Title Massaging" as a deceptive practice. To them, it doesn't matter that the work you did doesn't match the job title. And it doesn't matter that you struggled under a job title that didn't accurately represent your responsibilities, either. They take exception when candidates assume job titles that they actually haven't held.

From a human resources standpoint, the job title on the résumé should absolutely match the one in the personnel file.

Anything different than what is listed on file isn't considered an official employment record.

However, if you feel that your job title is so far out in left field from the realities of your daily work, there IS hope in trying to correct someone's impression of your background.

Keeping in mind that you need to always take the higher ground and provide the actual title of the job that you held, you can provide some insight as to the equivalent that best represents the level at which you were functioning.

Here's how:

Company Name – City, ST
Actual Title (equivalent to _____)

Another problem area: People also try to "lump" the entirety of their career at a particular company under the highest job title that they held, rather than separately listing each position with the start and end dates. In a way, this common practice is "stretching" how a person's work experience appears in a particular position.

You ALWAYS want to honest, and more importantly, accurate in your résumé. Anything less could hurt your career by your being seen as dishonest.

KNOW WHEN TO CALL IN THE "BIG GUNS" FOR HELP

Not everyone has extra money lying around, especially when they are unemployed, to hire a professional résumé writer or other professional career service provider.

But in the long run, hiring an expert who can impartially "slice and dice" your background to find elusive nuggets when you can't see the forest for the trees is an investment in shortening your job search substantially.

Professionals help job seekers having:

- Trouble getting the proper voice and "résumé lingo" down.
- Difficulty trying to figure out which accomplishments to highlight.
- Formatting issues - not knowing how to strategically use white space and design elements to create a résumé that "pops".
- Limited time to spend on the document (or no desire to do it themselves).
- A need for a third party to objectively plow through the job seeker's background and clarify/define top value and accomplishments.
- Little idea on how to build an effective marketing strategy to position themselves competitively.
- Fear or insecurity in writing the résumé themselves, including lack of understanding about the strategy behind the document.
- Poor writing skills/abilities.
- Shyness about discussing their accomplishments.

Before hiring a professional writer or career services provider, check them out and make sure that they have taken the step to make you feel comfortable about their level of professionalism. It's about you, remember?

Did the writer join a professional résumé writing organization, and are they involved in their industry? Do they have any writing certifications? Those are telling signs as to whether this is someone you want to do business with, and also what you might expect if you book their services.

When it boils down to it, hiring a professional résumé writer really divides people into two groups. Some people see it as a cost (or expense) versus those who see it as an investment. The "cost" people see it as not what is being given to them, but instead, what is being taken from them: money. They already don't see the value of having someone else help them.

Conversely, the investment perspective creates a means to an end. One résumé writer recently gave a perfect example illustrating this: A) Invest $200 with a professional writer and get hired in two months – OR – B) Write your own, get hired in six months and spend $5,000 of your savings in the process.

This document has to be a well-thought out and deeply strategized marketing piece that tells a prospective employer your story and provides a compelling reason to hire you.

Résumé writers do this day in and day out, and have a solid handle on how to approach building this document's strategy and incorporating the appropriate lingo and positioning.

This process is never a one-way street. Résumé writers absolutely rely on their clients to provide important feedback to help shape the direction and add to the value of the résumé. It's a partnership... and the "cost" folks don't understand this aspect either.

RECOMMENDATIONS FROM AN EXPERT:
Top 5 Things Job Seekers Don't Know About Their Résumés

Susan Britton Whitcomb, author of *"Résumé Magic,"* is widely regarded as one of the top résumé writing gurus in the careers industry. As an expert in all the technical, aesthetic, and formatting specifics of writing these documents, here are the top 5 mis-steps she sees job seekers making when preparing their résumé:

- *Making the résumé the centerpiece of the job search.* This may have been true a decade ago, but it is no longer today. Far too many job seekers hyper-focus on the résumé, leading it as the first point of introduction, tweaking and re-tweaking it, and indiscriminately submitting it to any posting that looks appealing. Why? It feels "safer" to sit behind the supposed safety of that sheet of paper rather than be out networking with the people who can refer or hire you.

- *Assuming employers care about ALL of your background.* Too many job seekers write obituary-style résumés - they include everything they've done throughout their career. The reality is that employers want the most relevant information (without glaring historical omissions, of course). You need to look like you are a perfect fit, and if your résumé doesn't confirm that, you can be sure that your competitor who does will get the interview. Why do jobseekers make this mistake? They haven't been taught that job search is marketing, and marketing is about conveying the benefits to the consumer, and benefits must be things that really matter to the consumer (the employer).

- *Leaving out numbers-driven accomplishments.* Most job seekers know they should include accomplishments in their résumés. But, to make those accomplishments really catch a hiring manager's attention, they need to convey numbers — before-and-after numbers that tie to your ability to contribute to profitability, efficiencies, and cost-savings. The fact that you include those numbers on the résumé not only proves you can do the job but assures the hiring manager that you know how your position fits into the strategic profit picture. Why do most résumés miss the boat on numbers-driven accomplishments? Job seekers often think that their work doesn't really lend itself to numbers-oriented accomplishments. Or, they have not been taught to tie their work performance to the organization's bottom line.

- *Underestimating the power of a drop-dead résumé.* Visual appeal is your first impression. It's the difference between striding into an interview well-dressed or bumbling in with stains on your shirt or food stuck in your teeth. A visually appealing résumé can elicit the "wow" effect—and that effect may just be the thing that tips the scales in your favor when it comes to getting screened in or even getting an offer. Why is visual appeal overlooked? 1) Job seekers don't have good examples of gorgeous résumés to realize how much better their résumés could look. 2) It takes creativity and experience to figure out ways to avoid paragraphs that are too long, bulleted lists that go on forever, formatting that is missing critical white space, and so on.

- *Omitting critical keywords.* Keywords are the bait that causes your résumé to be plucked out of a sea of competing résumés. And, even if you don't submit your résumé online, it still needs keywords that create a connection when live human beings read it. The best way to determine which keywords to use is to extract them from descriptions within the job postings you're applying for. Why are keywords omitted so often? Many job seekers aren't familiar with the process employers use to locate potential candidates within résumé databases and applicant tracking systems. The more keyword matches you make, the better your chances of being considered for an interview.

COVER LETTERS

Should you send them? Yes. Do employers read them? Yes... and no. The part that hurts the most is that you can't definitively know who does read them and who doesn't. But the heart of the issue is that including a cover letter is an expected business formality. If you don't include one and the person accepting applications expects a cover letter, then you have just torpedoed your candidacy.

The truth is that during the first "pass" on all the applications, employers do not read cover letters, opting to get right to the meaty résumé first, but for the documents that are selected for a second look, the cover letter is

Cover Letters That Get Noticed Have:

- Complete applicant contact information
- Date
- Address line (personalized to hiring manager if possible)
- Separate line stating name of target position
- Salutation (formal)
- Hook (to get their attention) – use quotes, hanging statements or other tricks to keep them reading
- Identification of employer need or pain point
- Relating your career assets to employer needs
- Making the case of how employer would benefit by hiring youActively closing the "sale" with follow up actions
- Thank you
- Applicant signature

The same contact information heading/format that you use in your cover letter should be the same as the one used on your cover letter... you are creating a personal look/brand for your marketing documents and should keep it consistent.

carefully reviewed and does factor into the overall candidate evaluation process.

But not having one could be devastating, especially if there is no personalized attempt on your behalf to introduce yourself to the employer and provide a compelling reason to hire you.

Don't forget that many companies using Applicant Tracking Systems (ATS) can and do count cover letter keywords. By not including one, you could be hurting the keyword "density" associated with your application submission.

When sending these supplemental documents, try to view your résumé as "the facts" and the cover letter as "the compelling reason to hire you" – don't simply regurgitate your résumé into the letter, but instead, try to think about how you can link the employer's needs to what you offer.

A good way of thinking about this is by demonstrating that you know and understand employer "pain points." What problems are they facing, and how does what you bring to the table help solve those problems? By using the problem-solution method, you'll be able to approach developing a value-oriented overview of how you can make a difference for that employer.

But be careful how you write this document. You should always use formal business writing and salutations with the appropriate prefix (Mr./ Ms./Mrs./Dr. etc.).

But writing the cover letter is also tricky because there's one thing that people really fail at doing, and that involves not being able to write to the audience.

Remember, the job application process is about *you*, but in reality, it is about *them*.

Before sitting down to write a cover letter, try to get yourself in the right mindset about your audience.

Here's a great way to gain perspective: Have you ever been at a cocktail party where you introduce yourself to someone you don't know, and then the whole conversation ends up being all about them... they blabber on and on about themselves? Pretty soon, your attention has tuned out just like a television with a fuzzy static screen.

When employers get cover letters that have an overuse of personal pronouns such as "I," "me," or "my" – they see this as a complete turnoff... they are experiencing the same scenario as the cocktail party... where the business just wants to cover their ears and say "la la la la" to block it all out.

Don't despair – you can and will write a good cover letter – just write it from the heart and think about what an employer is going through... then connect how your background and assets will help.

REFERENCES

One of the most neglected areas of any working professional's job search tool kit is the list of updated personal and professional references. These are considered a critical instrument to your career success because an employer is seeking some kind of verification of your character, skills, personality, abilities, knowledge, and background.

But be aware that unless an employer asks you to submit these references as part of the application process, only send what they ask for... many hiring managers get frustrated when they ask for a simple résumé and cover letter and instead get references, portfolios, work examples, and recommendation letters. My advice is to play it just like you did back in school: follow the instructions. If the employer asks for it, send it. If they don't ask for it, don't send it.

One common mistake people make is to include "References are available upon request" on the bottom of their résumé. DON'T! This is redundant for the very reason if an employer asks for references, you will obviously provide them. Don't waste precious résumé space confirming something that is already an implicit expectation from a prospective employer.

It should also be noted that you do not need to include (in your work history section for each job you have worked) all the names of supervisors, phone numbers, or addresses of companies. That information is easily searchable online and comes across as insecure... like you are desperately trying to justify yourself and validate your work history. Only provide complete contact information for those people that you are actually listing as a reference.

When it comes down to listing your references, you should always have a separate sheet of paper with your references with you when you go to an interview. The formatting should be the same as your résumé and cover letter to maintain consistency in the look and feel of all of your career materials.

People who are proactively on top of their career tools are the ones that always have their reference list ready to go... before they even start a job search.

However, let's face it: friends and your personal/professional references do have certain "seasons" – what might be a strong connection now may fade with time, so you need to think about keeping your reference list current with your strongest supporters and advocates.

Job references are actually your biggest cheerleaders and are the ones that you pick to speak favorably on your behalf. These people must be chosen carefully and strategically. It may seem appropriate to appoint one of your closest friends, but how do they present themselves? Are your friends in positions of authority? Are they good communicators? Can they quickly, concisely, and enthusiastically endorse you?

Choose your reference list with your next job in mind. Tap into previous employers, mentors, supervisors, co-workers, counterparts, colleagues, and industry partners who know you best.

Then select each person based on what they can highlight about you... one person might have better knowledge on your character, while another reference could speak to your career expertise. You definitely don't want to have each of them addressing the same points about you... the most important thing to do when selecting references is to think about how each of them can say the same good things about you but in different perspectives.

For an example, after forwarding the job description for which you are applying, you should call each person on your reference list and coach one individual to talk about your character, another contact should talk up your skill sets, and another person can focus on your leadership. This provides a broader and deeper perspective of what you are "all about" to potential new companies.

But more importantly, the people who are on your reference list are people that you have actually asked. Don't "surprise" someone by not telling them you put them on the list, only to have an employer doing a reference check call them and catch them unaware of your new career purpose. That doesn't usually end well!

People who are excellent career managers maintain an active reference list of people with whom they have strong, vibrant connections. They do this by staying in touch with each person, and if there is a job interview in the works, the candidate coaches each job reference on talking up a unique aspect so the references all don't talk about the same thing.

By cultivating a list (separate from your résumé) of job references both personal and professional, you have proactively assembled your biggest cheering section that will do the best job in selling you to prospective employers.

What An Excellent Reference List Looks Like

Personal	**Professional**
Name	Name, Title
Address	Company
Phone * Cell * Email	Address
How you know them:	Phone * Cell * Email
	How you know them:

The general rule of thumb is to have an even number of personal vs. professional references, with at least two of each type to balance out.

Recommendations/Testimonials

Similar to references, recommendations and testimonials can have strong effects on your viability as a candidate. Collecting positive comments from customers, colleagues, co-workers, or bosses can actually be a nice feature to add to your résumé when appropriate. (It also goes without saying to ask for their permission to use their comments as a quote just so there aren't any ugly surprises later.)

Incorporating short quotes can break up blocky résumé text but more importantly, transfers credibility from the people being quoted to you. If a president of a company or a well-known thought leader agrees to provide a positive comment about you, this can serve as an endorsement to your application, and can have a significantly favorable impact to target audiences.

Testimonials are also very positive – we will talk about LinkedIn in an upcoming section, but by garnering testimonials on this popular networking site, this can provide anyone perusing your profile online with a 24/7 public affirmation of your integrity, expertise, abilities, leadership, and positive contributions.

Remember this important point: If someone tells you that you were helpful or provided a valuable service, don't be afraid to ask for them to put that into writing.

Career management means that you understand how to leverage compliments, kudos, testimonials, and recommendations as outside perceptions of what you bring to the table. We all know we are fabulous, but when someone else says it, it has a lot more impact because they are "tooting" the proverbial horn on our behalf.

SOCIAL MEDIA PROFILES

One of the harshest realities of job seeking today and managing one's career is that embracing technology is becoming an absolute. Those that refuse to embrace it risk becoming part of the digital divide and are regarded by a growing number of companies as obsolete. Technology is driving a lot of workplace innovations, and by some job seekers failing to embrace social media sends a strong signal to potential employers that there is a skill disconnect.

In short: If you aren't out there, they can't find you. Or even worse, if you don't show up in search results, companies could interpret this to mean that you are a "nobody" who doesn't even pop up on the radar screen.

With these rules of thumb in mind, it has become a necessity to build online social media profiles in order to register a "hit" or "ping" on employer searches.

There are multiple resources out there on all the steps involved in building effective and robust online profiles… but the key is that you absolutely need to be represented. LinkedIn, Facebook, Twitter, blogs, and Google+ are all great places to start. This will help you formulate an online career management strategy and put it into action.

Take the time to learn the platforms, fill them out completely, and keep them updated. It's not as time-consuming as you think. Yes, it will initially be a big investment, but once you complete the set-up, you'll usually only need to post quick, regular updates that are easier to handle.

From a career management perspective, building social media profiles requires two things: keeping the personal brand that you have developed intact as well as consistent, and using the social media channels in a professional fashion.

Everything you say publicly can either reinforce your positive brand or cause significant damage. In my own profiles, I always keep things "professionally personal" meaning that I would never post anything that could hurt my brand but at the same time, I like to add a touch of my personality so people know there isn't a robot sitting at the keyboard.

4

MISSION CONTROL, WE HAVE IGNITION

LAUNCHING YOUR JOB SEARCH

"Let every man be occupied, and occupied in the highest employment of which his nature is capable, and die with the consciousness that he has done his best."
- Sydney Smith

It's never an easy task to leave the reassuring routine of what we know and take a leap into the unknown. There's a certain amount of comfort knowing that if we are currently working that if we decide not to leave, we still have a job. But having time to find the right opportunity is a luxury that the jobless simply don't possess. For them, the stakes are much higher and have even greater urgency.

Because there is no such thing as job security, it is paramount that you do everything you can to prepare yourself in the event a job opening of interest comes your way, an opportunity for career advancement is offered to you, or an unplanned job transition wreaks havoc on even the best-laid career plans.

Active career management means being at the ready and prepared to handle each in a proactive manner… as opposed to scrambling at the last minute. By possessing a clarity of purpose and direction, you will have improved flexibility and responsiveness versus being behind the "eight-ball" which will set you back.

INTERNAL PROMOTIONS

Internal promotions or offers to advance your career within the same company don't happen by accident. Someone, somewhere along the way, took notice of you and understood your value proposition and contributions to the company to match those attributes to the open opportunity.

While this situation isn't quite being handed an opportunity on a silver platter, the moment when it arrives is actually a culmination of several contributing factors.

- **Positive attitude.**
Never, ever let them get you down. Once you lose control of your attitude, everything can come crumbling down around you. Move in active career management mode by remembering and making it a core value to always be positive in the workplace. One of the key reasons people get promoted is that they are pleasant to work with… at least in theory.

If you are dealing with a negative environment that makes you feel down about things, you need to force yourself into finding the silver lining.

Once you accept the negativity from the workforce into your mindset, you'll have a tough job selling yourself as a top choice for a promotion. Identify the areas that set off your "hot" buttons, and work to find ways to circumvent those emotions these issues elicit so you don't build up a bad attitude about work.

Another way to project positivity is to smile. Have you ever heard of smiling as a contagious disease? It's true. Try this on the street to random strangers (where appropriate, of course): Make eye contact, and smile. Most of the time, people will smile back. It's a natural reaction, and it also leaves the other person with a sense of positivity.

How you project yourself with positivity and enthusiasm is what gets noticed by supervisors.

- **Don't do just the minimum required to do the job.**
Employers value staff that are energized and passionate about what they do... this can mean increased productivity levels and innovation. By stepping up to shoulder additional responsibilities, lead specific projects, or brainstorm new ways to improve division or company operations, you are subtly establishing yourself as someone with a great deal of initiative. You can learn a lot of things along the way which can position you as someone who has the knowledge as well as capacity to go to the next level.

- **Cultivate a good connection with your supervisor.**
You don't need to butter up the boss, but you should make sure that you maintain a good connection. A good way to do this is through regular communications. One thing that really irks supervisors is when they have to try and extract project status updates from employees... if you voluntarily provide detailed updates on a regular, consistent basis, the supervisor will appreciate knowing where you (and the project) stand in terms of progress towards goal. By default, you are making their job easier by making yourself easier to manage.

- **Indicate interest.**

Workers hoping for a promotion often fail to communicate their interest in a position, only to find out that they have been passed over because management wasn't even aware of their interest. Chalk this up to a missed opportunity because the worker didn't get their hat in the ring to even be considered. By building relationships with key decision makers, you can make sure you are in tune with upcoming opportunities and find the right time to make your interest known.

- **Communicate your wins.**

Forward kudos to supervisors with a little note about the unique challenge that you encountered in completing a particular project – this helps validate your contributions to the company and how others see you. Also keep track of your results to benchmark your own performance metrics.

- **Be a proactive problem solver.**

A great way to get noticed internally is be helpful. Coming up with solutions to team problems or challenges to projects is an incredible way to catch the attention of bosses. It shows initiative by propelling the organization forward through effective issue resolution, and demonstrates leadership thinking.

- **Keep adding to your body of knowledge.**

In the résumé section of this book, it was discussed the importance of adding to your area of expertise and how employers can see this as invaluable. Being a helpful fountain of knowledge and resource will also help establish your internal authority and expertise.

- **Compliment others.**

This doesn't mean that you go around the office showering people with empty platitudes, but a well-placed and heart-felt compliment to someone on your team who has done a good job can win people over ... who then can become your biggest advocates and fans.

- **Build goodwill.**

Sometimes "taking one for the team" can mean a short-term loss but long-term gain. It might mean doing something you don't like, but it earns you "brownie points" with the audiences that matter. Whatever and whenever you can, you should always think about ways to foster goodwill among your stakeholders, customers, co-workers, and managers.

Deliberately and authentically exhibiting these tactics with your current employer is a great way to get noticed and attract the attention of company leaders to be considered for greater levels of responsibility.

JUMPING SHIP

Making the decision to leave an employer is never an easy one. There are a lot of things to consider – but one thing is for sure: there is no guarantee that any new job will work out better than your current one.

Job seeking is always a best-guess scenario – you are taking the leap of faith that a new job will deliver on everything that you hope. Most of the time, once you get on board, things are exactly as they seemed in the interview, but there are always those cautionary tales of horror that are the stuff of urban legend of leaping from the frying pan and into the fire... bad bosses exist and sometimes you don't know you've walked into one of these nightmares until it's too late.

The old axiom of "Never leave a job until you have the next one lined up" holds true, however. It is much more difficult to look for work when you are unemployed than while you are actually working.

Before the interview began, Ed sensed that the job candidate was a job-hopper.

But that also puts some pressure on you as the job seeker because suddenly, the time window that you have to look for other opportunities is compressed into short spurts... either during break times, lunches, or before/after work.

You should NEVER look for a new job while at your current job – by this I mean you shouldn't be using your current employer's resources to surf job sites, logging in on the office Wi-Fi with your own laptop, using your work email to respond to job openings, or giving out/using your work phone as a contact number.

One of the most critical mistakes employees looking for a new job make is by assuming that their activities are flying under the radar. More employers (than you think) are using spyware and keystroke software to track employee productivity levels and potentially look over your shoulder at the content you are producing. And to whom you are sending it.

REAL-WORLD EXAMPLE
Josh worked at a company of 35 employees and was shocked when he was at a conference and overheard his boss boasting to another industry leader that all the office computers had been loaded with spyware to keep track of employee activity. The supervisor said that the software was installed under a pretext of a regular update of the office system, so no one had a clue. As it stood, Josh had gotten lazy about using his own personal email account to email friends, and had been sending a lot of messages out through his work account. He was stunned and immediately stopped using his work account for *any* personal correspondence.

Many companies have some kind of employee manual that must be signed upon hire which addresses the rules governing the use of company property; violating those rules could be grounds for immediate dismissal. Because you never know who might be "watching," your job search should be on your personal time using your own resources.

Making the tough decision to leave an employer can be rooted in any number of reasons: maybe you can't stand your boss, the scope of work has changed or grown from where it was when you first got hired, you got bored, or perhaps you heard about that dream job opening that got your pulse racing.

These are some key indicators that it might be time for you to move on to another employer.

- **Your gut tells you to go and you are afraid to stay.**
ALWAYS listen to your instincts. You can usually count on the fact that they are dead-on. Trust me!

- **The boss keeps making promises to you, but never delivers.**
Sometimes, it is a ploy to keep you around by dangling a tantalizing promise that never becomes attainable. Other times, it is simple matter of economics… the money simply isn't there to make it pencil out financially. Either way, if the promises keep coming and they don't make good on the promise, it's a dead-end road.

- **Things are bad now and chances are that you'll be the one to blame later.**
Some companies unfortunately thrive on finding a single scapegoat to hang the blame on, fire that person, then move along. If you can see the clouds gathering, it's time to get your "move groove" on!

- **The office is ruled by a moody boss.**
If you are suffering under a boss whose mood swings change faster than most people change socks, you are probably walking around on egg-shells, and completely stressed out. It's not an easy thing to constantly have to adapt and predict what's going to happen next. And you shouldn't have to, either!

- **You aren't growing any more.**
If you have completely capped out responsibility, salary, and professional development-wise, you are in a career-ending stall-out and falling fast.

Time to reboot your engines and find a new job where you are energized and motivated again.

- **There's a revolving staff door.**

If co-workers are coming and going at a fast pace, that could also signal a core incompetency by the employer, or even worse, really bad management and/or employee morale. Sure, you could hunker down to keep your nose to the grindstone, but there will likely be a point in time where you will be caught in the crosshairs. Why linger and wait for the inevitable to happen?

- **Lots of closed-door meetings by senior management.**

This is a sure sign that something big is afoot. Being aware of how the company is performing budget-wise and how sales are compared to goals is important so you know where the business stands fiscally. Again, listen to your intuition. If things are feeling dicey, and everyone is getting skittish like deer during hunting season, this might be your cue.

- **You are unhappy.**

Sometimes, a variety of factors add up to a general sense of unease and dissatisfaction. Maybe you were passed over for a promotion. Or a co-worker keeps taking credit for your work. Maybe you feel unstimulated or unchallenged. If you aren't happy, chances are you aren't being as productive as you were back when you were still in love with the job.

- **Company's reputation has become tarnished.**

There have been any number of high-profile scandals and lawsuits in the media lately, and the stigma attached to those companies can have a negative impact on your employability. Potential employers often don't stop to think about you as the individual job seeker; sometimes they see guilt by association simply by virtue of your having worked at the company in question. If things are looking bad for your current employer, it's a good time to move on before the "you-know-what" really hits the fan!

- **You crave work with meaning; your life priorities have changed.**

Many baby boomers now are experiencing this painful moment in their careers where they realize that the work that they have been doing is not in alignment with their core values. What they are getting paid to do suddenly isn't anything that they enjoy. It might be time to launch an encore career that transfers skill sets into an entirely different field. Other times, people's circumstances change and what was important before (career advancement) isn't the most important driving factor... job satisfaction is instead.

- **You bring work home with you...as a monkey on your back.**

If you have been so stressed at work that you are getting physically ill or suffering mentally, it's time to bail from that job. The long-term effects of such high stress levels simply aren't worth it. Many people who have switched from a high-paying, high-anxiety job to lower paying, more mellow employment consider the trade-off completely worth it. It depends on what levels of stress you are willing to accept, and what the costs might be if you decide to stay.

There are a myriad of reasons to consider leaving a position... either because a great offer came your way or you have run into obstacles that stand in the way of you achieving your career goals. Making the decision to jump ship needs to be rooted in factual as well as emotional reasons... all well thought-out and not made in the heat of the moment so you have the ability to rationally make decisions towards long-term career gains.

Being Laid Off

Nothing stings and hurts more than being laid off or terminated. It leaves you with a bad taste in your mouth. You are angry. Hurt. Shell-shocked. The implicit message we get when this happens is that we have failed in some way. As a result, someone made the decision to take away our livelihood, which is something we all associate very closely to personally, spiritually, and professionally.

"Though we have to lay you off, our severance package, a carton of macaroni and cheese and a voucher for $25 at the snack machine, should help."

CREDIT: Special reprint permission from
John McPherson from "Close to Home" for use in this book

Getting through the layoff is your main goal; if you start seeing warning signs that one is imminent, then you need to get your own house in order.

- Update your résumé and make sure you review all the records needed to quantify your accomplishments… while you still have access to them.
- Always have at least 6 months of wages saved up as a cushion. There is no way to guess how long you might not have any income.
- Pay off as many debts as you can while you still can do so. Later, you'll be grateful to not have those obligations adding to your stress level.
- If you are offered a severance package, negotiate hard for the best deal. This is what you will need to survive on until your next job.
- Determine whether your unused vacation days can be cashed out.
- Take care of all of your loose ends – many people who are being laid off take advantage of being on more generous company medical plans to take care of regular health checkups before having to pay out-of-pocket insurance costs.
- Find out how any kind of medical coverage can be continued, if that is offered.
- Start thinking strategically about where you can go from your current job – what are the potential connecting points? Then start networking towards those areas.
- Before your last day, ask for a letter of recommendation. If the company is already undergoing layoffs, it may be in bigger financial trouble and not around for much longer. Get those endorsements while you still can!
- Never cash in your retirement accounts – unless you are facing going out on the street. Most people forget that they end up paying substantial penalties for early withdrawal on retirement accounts PLUS the regular taxes, which can eat up to 40-50% of the entire balance.

After the layoff, launching a job search is probably going to be one of the toughest things you'll ever have to do… because it means that you have to literally pick up the pieces of your shattered work life, try to pull yourself together, and then march on like nothing ever happened… even though you just went through one of the most humiliating and demoralizing experiences in your life.

However, before you start looking for a job, you need to work through your feelings. It's okay to be upset and angry, at first. You are still reeling from the impact and trying to process exactly what happened. And that takes time to work through all of those emotions.

But you CANNOT carry feelings of resentment or hostility into a job search.

Being angry will quickly and silently kill your viability as a job candidate. Until you have resolved the pain and accepted the situation, it is highly likely that you will wear your feelings on your sleeve for everyone to see, whether you know it or not.

Oftentimes, this comes out during interviews where some barb or snide comment about a previous employer surfaces. The person interviewing you will take notice.

Dealing with a sudden job loss is not an easy task.

You absolutely must take the time to mourn the loss of your job. Set up a counseling appointment. Get your emotions out into the open and examine them. You'll learn to accept what happened, and decide how you will handle those questions about your previous employer.

Being aware of how you answer questions about previous employers and how handle yourself during those tense moments can absolutely determine your career fate. Be kind to yourself before launching a career search by taking the time to process those powerful emotions which can shape your career destiny.

HOT COMMODITY: BEING RECRUITED

There is no bigger ego-boosting experience than to be actively courted by an employer who would like to add you to their staff. It is okay to revel briefly in feeling so desired – it is the highest compliment, after all.

The best way to handle being pursued by a company is to do your due diligence. If you don't know who they are, research the business thoroughly. Then tap into your network to find out what the "ground level" intelligence is on the business. What is the culture like? What challenges are they facing? What are the opportunities? The more you know, the more informed your decision.

Be thorough in your research and exercise caution about situations where you are being recruited as a "Lone Ranger" to ride in and rescue the company.

Some employers are so desperate for some kind of forward momentum after idling in the economic doldrums that they try to recruit new staff that will bring new credibility to the company image.

Other places are looking for a sacrificial lamb to bring in long enough to blame failure on, then fire them as a way to solve the problem.

Some companies simply place too many expectations on you.

Ask lots of questions. An important one is to find out exactly why you came to their attention and what attracted them to you as a candidate. Ask them how they think you will solve their needs and why. This will

ANSWERING QUESTIONS ABOUT A LAYOFF/TERMINATION

After you have handled the emotional upheaval brought on by the termination, you need to spend some time strategizing how to talk about it when in a job search. This part can and will have some kind of impact on your career destiny.

Write down 6 positive things that happened during your time during at that employer. It could be a "win" that you had on a project, or a client who appreciated your extra effort.

1._____   4. _____

2._____   5. _____

3. _____   6. _____

Now think about 3 valuable on-the-job lessons you learned at the company.

1._____   2. _____

3. _____

If you can shift your thinking away how hurt you are from what the previous company did "TO" you, and focus on what the company did "FOR" you, you will reshape your attitude. Any prospective employer wants to know if you made a mistake at previous company whether you learned from it or not, or if you have any other positive takeaways. You need to figure out these ahead of time because if you get into an interview session and can't come up with anything nice or positive to say, the company will assume that your previous employer was right in letting you go, especially since you seem like you have sour grapes. This is your opportunity to OWN your reason for a previous employer dismissing you emotions which can shape your career destiny.

give you better insight on their needs and problems so you have more clarity in the decision process… this can make the difference of accepting an offer or not.

If you are looking for a job, it is also critical to remember that you do not view a recruiter as not someone to overlook (or an "obstacle") between you and the company where you want to work.

Recruiters should be treated just like the human resources manager or hiring manager, because their client company has hired them to find and make a recommendation for talent acquisition. Too often, job seekers treat recruiters as annoyances and not like the key decision makers that they are, and end up getting on the recruiter's bad side as a result.

Many job seekers think that in order to find another job, all they have to do is contact a recruiter who will then go to work for the candidate to find them work. Unfortunately, it doesn't work that way. Recruiters do not work for you; they work for the company that hired them… and should never be seen as a person who will go to the ends of the earth to find you a job.

Instead, think of recruiters as valuable job search partners that you need to get to know, and treat them as decision makers who can act on your behalf when recommending you as the top candidate choice. Because that's what they really are!

GOING FISHING: WHERE THE JOBS ARE

Without the luxury of a gung-ho company or recruiter pursuing you for a specific position, ramping up a job search usually means trying to find out where the jobs are – which is often a very frustrating and confusing process.

Looking for work is one of the most ego-battering experiences... rejection is common and often becomes something that starts to feel personal as periods of unemployment grow longer.

An effective job search means having a polished, honed résumé, targeted job search that is in line with the résumé, and by networking, networking, and networking. You simply can't sit at home at the computer and hit "send" 84 times and expect results. Not in this day and age.

Going fishing where the jobs are means you need to get out of the house.

If you find yourself in the dreaded "5 C's" – which is sitting on the Couch with the Curtains Closed, eating Cheetos and watching CNN, then this is your wakeup call.

You need to get up, get dressed, and get out of the house. Networking doesn't fall in your lap; you have to work at it... it's a long process that can be daunting for some. But then again, nothing worthwhile is ever easy, is it?

Here are some tips to start building up your contacts:

- **Networking events.**
Networking is where you need to spend your time in order to yield the results that you seek. Career industry experts report that somewhere around 70-80% of all jobs are found through someone you know, so being passive and not being your own job search advocate is a guaranteed dead-end in a job search.

Scared of networking?

You must get over it… this doesn't mean that you have to be a smooth mover and really work over a room.

If you approach every networking event as an opportunity to start conversations or a place to meet interesting people, the pressure will be off. Just relax and have fun.

Do you hate speaking to people? Or do you get nervous?

Join a Toastmasters club to gain confidence in your speaking and people skills – they offer a supportive learning environment which will help you increase your presentation proficiencies and come across as a smoother networker. You may not feel that way on the inside, but you will have enough confidence to at least be effective in person.

REAL-WORLD EXAMPLE

On a personal note, I can relate to not feeling comfortable networking. When I was a little kid, I was a shy stutterer – almost to a stuttering level equal to that of Porky Pig. Fortunately, my grandmother pushed me to get involved in my high school speech team where I entered the oratory (8-minute memorized speech) category. In college, I joined the debate team and from there, I have slowly overcome my shyness and learned how to network the room.

Sometimes, it is as simple as sticking out your hand to greet someone, and starting the conversation with, "Hi, my name is _____. What brings you to this meeting?" Usually, that gets the other person talking and takes the weight off of you to manage and guide the conversation.

If you are at an event that is industry-related, usually you will have a lot to talk about and share. If you have kept up with trade magazines and business journals, this will also provide conversational fodder to keep things moving.

The real trick to networking for jobs is to think of it as a business conversation and that you are there to meet friends. In my hometown of Portland, Oregon, Cleon Cox III leads a job seeker support group and has a famous saying that truly sums it up for job seekers when it comes to going to networking events: "Have fun, meet new people, and learn something."

If you stop thinking of networking events as a pressure cooker where your future employability hangs in the balance, you'll relax and have a much better experience.

- **Informational interviews.**

Informational interviews are actually networking… with a purpose. But you might be surprised to learn that the purpose is actually NOT to ask for a job. It's all about gathering information. If someone is willing to grant you time for a face-to-face / sit-down meeting or a phone call, consider this a golden gift. It is an opportunity to mine for information about company culture, job requirements, recommended career steps, and a way to identify any skill gaps that can be remedied through professional development. If you play your cards right and impress the person (don't forget to send a thank you note for their time!), you could win over a job search advocate. Their company might not be hiring, but this person might be connected to someone at the company who might be at some point.

Informational interviews + networking = an ever-widening spider web in which you will eventually snare a job lead that will lead to your hiring.

- **Business publications.**

I am a big advocate of either subscribing (or going to the library) to read local business publications, which are goldmines of information if you know how to use them properly. Business journals in most major metropolitan cities often have articles about companies winning over venture capital or announcing expansion plans. Additionally, there usually is some kind of a "People On the Move" section detailing recent hires for local companies. I see that as practically screaming unadvertised job openings... at each person's previous employer. Finally, new business licenses and property transactions can signal new openings and company growth plans before jobs are even announced.

- **Alumni/affinity groups.**

The power of association can weight your application or interest in a job favorably with someone else who shares that affiliation. Joining online alumni or affinity groups can also reveal "member-only" opportunities with preferences given to those who share that same connection.

- **Google alerts.**

This is incredible tool which you can set up to deliver a daily digest of specific keywords including job titles. Google scours the web and sends you a compilation of incidents where new content appears with those keywords. This can capture job openings as well as mention of personnel shifts.

- **LinkedIn.**

This online platform has become vital to job seekers in two ways: Employers like the "Six Degrees of Separation" to see how you might be connected to their current employees, and because of this, some companies are ONLY using LinkedIn to post jobs so there is a "known quantity" to your application. Conversely, many HR and recruiting companies are scouring LinkedIn using keywords to source talent... which means you absolutely need a robust, complete profile up so when you appear in search results, the information will compel them to read further and ultimately contact you.

LinkedIn is great for connecting to people and networking, but always take the time to personalize your messages to people you don't know when requesting to connect with them... using the standard default greeting is a fast way to getting your inquiry ignored. You only have one chance to make a good impression, so use the information you have gathered through reading industry and business publications as your opening line. As in, "Congratulations on (company name)'s new expansion – just read about that in (publication name). If you have 10 minutes, I would love to treat you to coffee to learn more!"

- **Join job support groups.**

Some people worry that groups like these are perennial gatherings of the chronically unemployed. You need to absolutely change that perception. Job support groups are a huge resource and are full of people willing to open up their networks and share job leads. If you decide to attend one of those meetings, be clear on what it is that you are looking for and also tune up your "elevator pitch" – you need to be succinct and specific when it is your time to share. Also be ready and willing to share your contacts as a good-faith contributor of the group.

- **Job board/online job ads.**

By the time that most jobs are posted online, there are already some serious candidates already under consideration. Many companies offer openings up internally first and then go outside of the business to fulfill hiring compliance requirements, or troll for even more qualified talent. Of course, there are still windows of opportunities for applying, and people do still find jobs this way, so you should go ahead and submit your application.

In reality, the real value in job boards and job ads is to track and watch company hiring activity... it's a great way to do a pulse check to see how the company is growing or changing by the numbers of jobs that are opening up. You can also use job announcements for positions you don't apply for to learn more about the company's operations and expectations for employees.

CLOSE TO HOME JOHN McPHERSON

"All I know is that we found him on Monster.com."

CREDIT: Special reprint permission from
John McPherson from "Close to Home" for use in this book

- **Job fairs.**

It is a rare occurrence to be hired on-the-spot at an actual job fair. Many companies use these fairs as a community relations opportunity, much to the disappointment of the people who have waited for hours to get in, only to find out that there were no positions available.

However, if you play your cards right, you can transform what could be a disappointing experience into a direct pipeline inside a target company.

Start by researching the company and uncovering what fit you see between your abilities and their needs. Make sure to scout their website and do a Google search to turn up any news articles that can provide additional information about the company's activities. Then, zero in on a specific job title and department, and make your move.

At the job fair, the person at the booth will likely be expecting you to shake their hand, fork over your résumé, chat a bit, then leave. Instead, if you see this as a chance to make an internal company contact that can refer you to the target department/hiring manager, you can tap into this face-to-face connection at the job fair as a stepping stone for connecting to your target person.

- **Industry/trade associations.**

Your best bet is to have clarity in your target job (see Chapter 1 on Career Purpose) and then concentrate your job search efforts in that specific arena. Many times, professional associations have their own job boards for their organization and member companies to post their openings. Doesn't it make sense to be focusing your energy and efforts on the right "pack" in which you should be running?

Cultivate these networks. Don't just send in your membership check and expect the phone to start ringing. You'll need to start attending events that the association or group puts on. A great idea to start building your networking quotient with the group is to volunteer to help with event registration. That way, you'll have an opportunity to meet every single person coming to the event and get to associate names and faces (and vice versa with them getting to know you)... which is a powerful networking tool!

- **Asking for SPECIFIC job search help/leads.**

One of the most neglected areas of a job search that could prove to be the most fruitful is when people looking for work actually *ask* for help.

Some people feel embarrassed about requesting assistance; they want to soldier on valiantly and not burden their network, or feel like their connections might think less of them.

That's the wrong mentality; instead, your network is there for a reason. You help them when they need it, and they return the favor.

But the only way that this will yield results is if you are *specific* in your request.

Simply sending out an "S.O.S." broadcast call for help along the lines of: "I need a job, any job" is totally useless.

Why? Because no one keeps a running tally of jobs just for you. That's what job boards do.

Here's a great example of what you should be doing instead of posting: "I need a job – please let me know if you have any leads."

Alternative ways to better phrase your job search request: (being specific)

- Including information about what specific job titles you are interested in
- Providing a little background on what it is that you specifically do
- Any geographical employment preferences (i.e. in a particular area)
- Short list of target companies you are concentrating your job search efforts on
- Requesting assistance in connecting to specific people at those target companies

Being vague is the fastest way to become forgotten when asking for assistance during a job search. If you can provide specifics such as, "I have been a marketing director and was recently laid off, so I am launching my job search and am specifically interested in jobs in the Portland, Oregon, area. Could you check your network to see if you know anyone at (target company name) company? I would greatly appreciate an introduction if possible so I can set up an informational interview."

This sounds so much better than: "Help, I need a job – will do anything" doesn't it?

- **Spring-boarding: be open to all options.**
Just because a job isn't full-time doesn't mean you shouldn't consider it. Think of it as a means to an end… you could use temporary or contract work (or even volunteering stints) to spring-board into a permanent job when one comes available. If you prove to be invaluable and the company's financial situation improves, you have just positioned yourself as the ideal candidate for the company to make a seamless full-time hire.

Using Social Media In Job Searches

New York might be the city that never sleeps but social media can be the job search agent that never sleeps. The Internet never closes for business and is out there, 24 hours a day, 7 days a week, 365 days a year. That means you can use it any time from practically anywhere to look for employment, but conversely, it means anyone at any time can use it to search for you.

Finding a job through social media and online networking is the fastest growing areas of the Internet. But there is one fundamental fact that remains unchanged between the "real life" and digital world: we are human and therefore we desire and create meaningful relationships with people that we like.

The amazing resources online have allowed us to find and connect to people that in all likelihood, we might not have run into on the street or at a local networking meeting. It is possible to build meaningful relationships but it does take a lot more effort because there has to be credibility to be attached to our online social personas.

If you are wondering where the jobs all are... you are thinking the wrong thing. You need to focus on the people who will lead you to where the jobs are.

The major social media sites have already been mentioned in this book: Facebook, Google+, LinkedIn, and Twitter. For your profile to even be considered, the ground rules are simple: Include a professional photo of yourself, fill out the profiles completely and as fully as possible, optimize the profile with relevant keywords for your industry/field, request to connect with contacts using not the default "request" but instead personalizing your reasons to connect (so they get to know you), and making sure what you post is personal yet professional.

It does take time to learn each platform and the nuances for each, but once you feel comfortable moving around in each of those sites, then you are ready to start a targeted job search.

Here are some strategies to use for each social media platform:

Blogging

- **Start one to establish subject matter expertise.** Employers hire subject matter experts and the best way to demonstrate this is to start a separate blog on WordPress or Blogger (there are many other platforms out there besides these two). This provides you an opportunity to write about what you know and highlight that expertise and your experiences.
- **Interview thought leaders.** You can leverage your blog as a way to reach out to specific individuals and give them a little ego boost by saying that you would like to interview them as a thought leader for your blog. That builds affinity and respect as well if you are producing high-level, useful content.
- **Encourage contacts to comment.** Instead of interviewing people, you can write a blog post then ask specific individuals what they think, encouraging them to leave a comment which opens the door to an engaging conversation.
- **Mention target companies and provide track-backs to their site.** Writing a post that is not effusive but mentions a target company in a positive light, then providing a link to their site is seen as a great way to make you look good for sending traffic their way.

LinkedIn

Building your profile:
I just got back from a presentation where I asked audience members to raise their hands if they were LinkedIn… and as usual, several people simply sat that question out… and avoided eye contact with me.

As a follow up, I then queried the group as to who had made their profiles robust and updated them recently. A large number of hands came down at that point. After the program was over, several people came up to me and said that they had a profile up but it wasn't something of which they were particularly proud, but they knew other LinkedIn users were looking at them, based on the stats.

My message?

WAKE UP! Don't be a LinkedIn "Ignoridiot!"

Folks resisting technology and plugging their heads into the proverbial ostrich hole and other people who just post up the minimal content are completely missing the boat.

Looking for a job? Many companies are only using LinkedIn to post employment opportunities to see how candidates might be linked to their company. But only people who are already LinkedIn users can apply, which means you are shut out of that process completely.

Not looking for a job? Many recruiters are prowling LinkedIn looking for industry talent. Don't you want to have your door open to these offers?

The point is that if you aren't on there, they cannot find you.

And what you post on this social media platform profoundly impacts how others see you. It is critical that you view LinkedIn as one of the main cornerstones of your career marketing materials much like you would view your résumé or cover letter.

But here's the catch:

LinkedIn is on all the time and anyone in the world can find you. And if you can't be found, then there's a major door to your career future that hasn't been opened yet.

Some people scoff and see LinkedIn and all new technology as a contrivance, but from everything I have heard, learned, and listened to from industry experts, it is false to believe that you can still be out there working and not have an active, completely filled out profile.

A careers industry colleague, Jason Alba, one of the country's top LinkedIn experts, recently provided a great example of a top-notch LinkedIn profile.

Here are some recommended strategies to avoid being a LinkedIn "Ignoridiot."

- **If you aren't on there, get on there.**
You are only hurting yourself and keeping yourself shut off from any and all opportunities.

- **Add a photo.**
Don't be a blank "egg" – humans are visual creatures. For your photo shoot, dress conservatively like you would for an interview. LinkedIn is like an interview that is available year-round, 24/7. However, don't high-tail it over to Glamour Shots. Please do make the best clean-cut appearance possible with minimal jewelry. You only get one chance to make a first impression.

- **Add a headline.**
Don't list "unemployed" because unemployed is not a direction. You want to point to the positive goal you are aiming towards, so create a job title headline. Then you can list that you are available underneath that.

- **Get a personalized URL.**
LinkedIn provides this option. It is a heckuva lot easier for an employer to type in your name than the lengthy default number, letter, and symbol URL that LinkedIn assigns.

- **Create a compelling summary.**

Saying that you are an "experienced blah blah blah manager" is NOT good enough anymore. This is social media, and that means adding a warm touch. Use this summary to convey a bit about your personality and unveil some of your passion for your field.

- **Add some bling.**

Make sure to add links that augment and enhance your profile. Use SlideShare to include a presentation that showcases your credentials. But whatever you do, make sure that the links that you include lead to useful, polished, and relevant information.

- **Include your specialties.**

(Pssst.... here's the secret: This is your keyword search area) Don't know what those are? Go to onetonline.org and type in your job title. Presto! Make yourself searchable.

- **Tell a story about each job record.**

Of course you are limited with the number of characters so you will only want to include the "biggies" about your accomplishments, but toss a bone to your former employer and make yourself look good: lead off with a story talking about the biggest takeaway and/or lesson you learned at that company. It's a win-win situation – you look generous, your previous employer looks good, and the potential employer feels like they have a future employee in front of them who is a learner and adapter.

- **Don't forget the awards.**

If you have any specific accolades in your field, make sure you list them. In essence, this is how you have separated yourself from the crowd.

- **Education.**

Besides the good old-fashioned book learning, leverage (if possible) what you learned in school and provide a good example of how you have been able to apply it in the real world. Employers love that! But please don't list what year you graduated – LinkedIn lets you choose the 'blank' option. This will help avoid potential age discrimination problems.

- **Volunteer.**

Being engaged and involved in your field or industry shows traction, commitment, integrity, and energy. Remember to keep track of these engagements.

- **Get recommended.**

By asking others to make a recommendation (no "scratch my back and I'll scratch yours"), you are actually leveraging their reputation to endorse you, which also gives you a boost in credibility. Think supervisors, former bosses, colleagues, mentors, industry partners, or subordinates. But please do not have your best pal or family members recommend you. Just don't.

- **Join industry groups.**

Keep on top of trends and share ideas… all very attractive things to employers hunting for new employees who are at the peak of their field/industry.

- **Update your status regularly.**

If you don't use your profile, how do you expect others to? Just remember, if the lights are on and no one is home, employers will move along to someone else who will answer the door.

Cultivating an active LinkedIn profile requires vigilance, persistence, and resolve. But by doing so, you avoid becoming an "Ignoridiot" and instead open the doors to who knows what kind of opportunity.

Looking for jobs on LinkedIn

- **Look up specific job openings at target companies.**

Many companies only post job openings on this website because they like having some degree of connection to potential candidates; as part of their extended network, you are a "known" quantity of sorts.

- **Find connections at target companies.**

Visit company profile online and seeing how you are connected through 1st, 2nd, and 3rd-tier connections. This information can be helpful for setting up informational interviews or personalizing cover letters when no contact information is provided in job postings.

- **Follow your target company.**

This function allows you to see any status updates that the company has posted, and can give you an inside scoop on upcoming initiatives and potential hiring moves.

- **Check out the news section.**

Similar to reading a business journal, LinkedIn created an aggregated news feed of members and companies so you can keep track of what companies are expanding, adding space, and ultimately, hiring.

- **Questions and Answers.**

Sometimes, you can attract the attention of companies by following questions and answers in this section of LinkedIn. By responding with a helpful, non-self-promotional answer, you can gain respect and possibly make some connections to target companies by building up online rapport.

- **Joining LinkedIn groups where contacts from your target groups frequent.**

Think of this as an "online" mixer. Figure out which relevant LinkedIn groups might be appealing to contacts from your target company, and do some lurking… are they there? Are they engaged? If so, join or request to join the group, and once admitted, follow the discussions. Your positive contributions can raise your profile within a very specific target audience, and be an opportunity to prove your value and expertise in a low-key way. You can demonstrate your expertise by providing useful information, but be careful about only dumping in your blog postings and leaving. That is truly poor form and does nothing to build up your brand.

- **Well-crafted polls can boost your visibility.**

Sometimes, while preparing for a job search, gaining some larger industry data through a survey can be very helpful. Putting together a short, concise, and outcome-driven poll and posting it in LinkedIn groups can be both innovative and help a job search simultaneously. You can post the poll in the target groups on LinkedIn (which can include the specific companies you are interested in), and engage them in taking a poll. They may be curious about your end results and could be a way that your information could open the door to future conversations.

- **Add to your reading list.**

Read a industry or business-related book and include this on your LinkedIn reading list... sometimes this can attract like-minded people while also demonstrating more activity on your profile that shows that you are interested in industry topics and trends.

- **Add your blog link.**

Linking your blog to your LinkedIn profile adds more content and robustness that backs up your industry knowledge. It also helps improve your online searchability.

Twitter

- **Create a handle that is industry-specific.**

You can also just use your name, but sometimes having a unique handle that incorporates your job title can help make you more searchable. Whatever you do, make sure it is a professional username.

- **Follow target companies and human resource departments.**
Many companies have separate main corporate Twitter feeds where you can keep up to date with current events going on with the organization, while the human resource department (for larger companies) oftentimes has a @(company name)Jobs username that is used to post job announcements.

- **Follow key company executives or decision makers.**
Depending on the organization, you may be able to follow individuals versus the company itself. If that is the case, follow them as a way to get to know the user.

- **Follow industry thought leaders.**
Sometimes, these folks provide unique insights or ideas that could help you approach a target company.

- **Favorite useful tweets.**
If your target Twitter user has some great Tweets, favorite them. That helps them look better to their audiences.

- **Create a positive list and add a user to it.**
Let's say you are excited about a particular business and add them to a Twitter list you created titled, "Top Companies to Watch" – they can see that you listed them there and are actually making them look good by holding them in such high esteem. This is a great way to catch their attention.

- **Send a note.**
If one of your targets posts a useful note or Tweet, send a quick message to them thanking them for the info. Or provide an answer if they post a question. The trick here is to engage on a regular basis and become a known quantity.

- **Ask for help in connecting.**
This is somewhat of a gutsy move and the worst thing that can happen is that they don't respond or say, "no." Reach out to the person or company

you are following and ask them, "Love your posts and find them useful. Would love to connect with (position title) at your company. Can U provide the name of that person?"

- **Post updates.**

Be active and engaged. Use TweetDeck or other Twitter-based platforms to schedule updates where you can provide tidbits of knowledge or advice. People follow helpful people, and you can quickly gain a good following by providing useful content.

Facebook

- **Beware of your content.**

Now that Facebook has launched the new "Timeline" feature, even more past content is easily dug up by anyone that you friend, or any administrator of any page that you like. Take the time to clean everything up and remove anything that might be found objectionable by a potential employer. "Personal yet professional" is a good mantra to follow when using Facebook.

- **"Fan" or "Like" target companies on Facebook.**

With this gesture, you are indicating that this company is one that you like which eclipses the fact that you simply like that they have a job open that you want. What better potential employee material than an enthusiastic brand ambassador? Also be aware that many companies are actually checking to see if a candidate has liked their company Facebook page to gauge that person's interest in the business… even before the interview.

- **Use your Facebook network to make connections.**

Referrals from friends or connections on Facebook to recruiters, hiring managers, or human resource contacts are powerful job search tools. If someone in your network has connections at your destination company, ask them to make an introduction on your behalf and connect on Facebook. This is a much more relaxed environment than more formal business introductions.

- **Join relevant Facebook groups.**

There are a lot of shared interest groups on Facebook and opportunities to join like-minded communities. Getting involved in relevant ones allows you to connect to the right people.

- **Create an ad seen by your target audience.**

Facebook ads are getting better in refining how they match ad content to user interests/preferences. Creating a simple ad composed of a professional photo of you and your short value proposition or a compelling statement can capture interest within your network. Think about how a lot of the headlines for online news services and offer enough of a teaser to inspire you to click and read further. That's what you need to do for your ad to get them to click on your LinkedIn profile or online portfolio.

- **Post updates so your social network knows what you are up to.**

Indicating that you just had an interview or applied for a job at a target company are great ways to keep everyone up to speed. You can also tag your friends in posts which will automatically give them an update as well.

- **Pull your blog feed into Facebook.**

This can be set up to feed into notes that get posted on your page which allows a greater audience to access your content, while boosting your SEO rating by having external links to the blog itself.

- **Use the Facebook instant message feature to get answers quickly.**

Sort of like sending a message over Twitter, this feature can allow you to see if anyone that you've friended at your target company is online and send them a quick message.

YouTube

- **Get found on the 2nd largest Internet search engine.**
Google is on top right now, but content is king, and people love video. But be careful about posting a video résumé if you aren't comfortable or familiar with creating online content.

A stiff, uncomfortable video presentation posted up on YouTube can do more damage than good, and also runs the risk of become fodder for viral videos if done poorly. Relax and consider doing some kind of back-and-forth interview to create a conversational effect, versus trying to face down the camera and look comfortable doing it.

Make sure you tag videos with appropriate and relevant keywords to your target audiences so when they use them as searchable terms, your content gets good return results.

- **Add favorites.**
You can like other YouTube content (including any that your target company has produced) to create a cloud around yourself that is relevant and highly focused on a particular industry, field, function, or business. This all adds to searchability online.

Smartphone Apps

- **Get jobs at your finger tips.**
You can use your smartphone to keep your social networks updated and there are specific apps you can download that will provide instant access to job openings. As mentioned previously, Mashable.com is a great resource that provides reviews and insights for the many new and emerging social platforms used on smartphones.

Hidden Jobs

There's a lot of buzz out there about all of the "hidden" jobs available. What exactly is the hidden job market and how can you access it?

Hidden jobs are obviously the ones that never get posted. The employer doesn't need to advertise these jobs because the talent is coming to them, versus the company looking for the talent.

Most career industry professionals agree that by the time a job position gets posted or advertised, in all likelihood, the employer already has a pretty good idea of who they want to hire. Sometimes, just posting the job is a mere formality. How many times have you sent in an application only to find out the position is no longer available?

Here are some tips to prepare yourself for tapping into the hidden job market.

- **Angle for internal promotions.**
We've already discussed how you need to proactively position yourself (if already inside a company) to be considered for advancement. But many times, these "hidden" jobs are ones that start internally first then move externally if the right candidate isn't found. Keep your supervisor involved in your work and let them know you are interested in moving up.

- **Network like a fiend.**
The days of having someone drop an awesome job in your lap are practically over. You need to be your own advocate and keep yourself out there. Everyone else is pulling out all the stops on networking which means they are at the front of the line to be considered for the job because the company already knows who they are, versus an unknown outsider.

- **Realize that deadlines are lies.**

With the exception of governmental or educational institutions, most application deadlines are absolute lies. They are arbitrary dates placed on an opening that in reality, are quickly filled long before the closing date.

REAL-WORLD EXAMPLE

"Sue" was interested in a job at a company for which she was well-qualified, but the closing date wasn't until Friday at 5 p.m. She took her time putting the application materials together, and drove over to the employer's office to drop them off before the deadline... at 4:45 p.m.

She waited and waited, but never heard anything. Finally she called, and found out that they had hired someone the Tuesday before the deadline.

From the employer's standpoint: The company isn't waiting until the stroke of 5 p.m. on Friday to suddenly rub their hands together with glee and say, "Yahoo; now I get to review all of these great résumés!" Instead, they are parsing through the résumés as they come in and when the business stumbles over a great document, they call that candidate right away.

- **Boost your own search engine optimization/visibility.**

Buying your own domain name and then claiming your own personalized URLs on social networks will help you be found and also control your social presence. Same for joining online directories. You need to exhaustively go through and get yourself listed. Commenting on discussions, posts, and answering questions on industry portals all add up to a greater 10,000-foot perspective and accumulation of positive content about yourself. The nice result from all of this initial work means that you have optimized your name and background to make it more search-friendly!

- **Teach a class or give industry presentations.**
While these directly apply to optimizing your search results, being someone who delivers content can catapult you into an entirely different universe and drive people looking for talent towards you. Don't overlook these opportunities if you are comfortable talking in front of groups!

HOW TO FIND HIDDEN JOBS

Actually penetrating the mist that shrouds hidden jobs requires patience and thorough research, but always remember that hidden jobs are found through people and companies, not in ads. And then be willing to be unconventional. Ask yourself how many other companies may not focus on your field specifically, but might also need the types of transferrable skills that you offer?

Many employers looking to shake up their current paradigm are interested in talking to candidates from outside industries for a fresh perspective. For example, a lawyer working at a firm might be able to transfer those skill sets into a non-profit or corporation needing legal counsel. Sometimes, the hidden jobs in these markets are all about leveraging a specific skill set from an entire industry and connecting them to a specific business need.

A lot of hidden jobs happen through being vigilant and simply watching trends. If you are paying attention to news articles and feeds, the key things that should set off your alarm bells are mentions of start-ups, company expansions, or businesses that have won significant contracts.

For example, in one short span in 2011, Insitu, a quickly growing defense-based company based in the tiny town of White Salmon, Washington, won several multi-million dollar contracts from the military for the unmanned aerial drones that they produce. Given the scale of the contracts, it is a very good assumption that the company will be adding personnel to grow their production capacity in accommodating those contracts.

Being alert for news items and terms relating to increases in profit, growth, expansions, funds raised, and wins are all things that should get you moving into contacting the business right now. Don't wait until the job is actually posted... you need to absolutely be the first person in line, not the last.

Another great place to tap into potentially hidden jobs is by reading the new business license listings in your local business journal. Most start-ups haven't gotten fully staffed yet, so using this weekly list as a way to prospect for potential future hiring needs could give you an opportunity to expose the company to your employment assets and even expose a hiring need they didn't realize they had.

Local business journals usually include a section that highlights people on the move. Watch to see who has moved from which company , and can raise a flag for you about a staff vacancy at the company they just left. This is the perfect time to make your move!

Informational interviews are also good ways to tap into a company. Remember, you aren't going in asking for a specific position; instead, you are gathering information. Your contact can reveal not-in-the-public-eye information about the company's initiatives and even provide accidental insight on where staffing needs may lie. This can help you start maneuvering towards a specific job before it even surfaces within the company consciousness.

You may have also heard of position proposals which are the direct result of your intimate knowledge of a specific company. You will need to have an internal advocate at that company who is willing to get you an appointment in front of the key decision maker where you can make your case for creating a new position with you as their top candidate choice.

This move requires a lot of confidence and enthusiasm, backed by rock-solid numbers and return-on-investment justification. An employer's first thoughts will be, "How much is this going to cost me?" but if you can provide a compelling case for hiring you that demonstrates profitability, they'll be listening more closely.

Another option for finding your way into hidden jobs could be, if you are unemployed, to start a consultancy. When there is no up-front hiring commitment to a long-term employee, sometimes employers are more apt to bring contractors in… which can be a proving ground for full-time, regular employment down the line after you prove your worth. It's a no-commitment trial run which can get you in the door while at the same time paving the way to a hidden full-time position when the employer is ready to create it.

Belonging to trade organizations or volunteering are great ways to find hidden jobs. By running with the right pack or already having an inside scoop on an organization, you'll hear of people leaving jobs… which comes before positions are actually posted. Oftentimes, there is a considerable delay if the departure is unexpected, so that provides a wide-open window for you to start marketing yourself to the decision makers before the job is opened up.

Finally, contacting someone that you admire could open future doors by motivating and activating them to act on your behalf. The key in this possibility is to build rapport with them by getting to know them… if they are local, invite them to coffee (your treat) or if you are traveling to their town, ask if you could stop by. Humans relish personal interactions and once we meet someone in person, we are more likely to try and help them. I recently met a well-known speaker who, since that meeting, has connected me to no less than 5 different top-tier people that were on my top list of people to meet.

Mobile Apps for Job Searches

In many cases, having instant accessibility to looking for jobs can make the difference for employers posting open positions without a prior candidate in mind. A post by Maisha Cannon on the highly-regarded website Recruiting Blogs provided an excellent list of apps that are considered "must-haves" for job seekers on the go who have a smartphone:

http://www.recruitingblogs.com/profiles/blogs/mobile-apps-to-help-manage-your-job-search

Job Search Plan

For unemployed people, keeping structured is the biggest challenge to a job search. Back when they were working, the office had a flow with deadlines, reports, and processes which provided that structure. Now, there suddenly isn't any, and people become disoriented… they know they need to be applying for jobs, following up on job applications, and networking, among some of the many recommended activities. All of these tasks can start to feel pretty overwhelming very quickly.

Pulling all of these methods into a coherent job search is always tough. Someone once told me: Looking for a job *is* a full-time job. People who are in charge of their career management absolutely adopt that mentality.

One of the biggest issues with launching a job search is keeping organized. Not keeping track of where you are and what you need to be doing is one of biggest reasons people end up getting burned out and frustrated during a job search.

There are many tools out there to track your productivity and results, including JibberJobber.com which is a great resource. Or you can simply set up a basic Excel spreadsheet to track everything. Most experts do recommend starting some kind of job search diary to organize your tasks and create goals so you add structure to your day.

If you are setting off on a job search, the most proactive thing you can do is to build a job search plan which you will use to hold yourself accountable. When you track your accomplishments to those goals, you will start to feel traction and also be able to see where your efforts are yielding the best results. It's entirely too easy to fall into a pattern of the "shotgun" approach by trying to do too much and ending up doing none of it well. Tracking then concentrating your efforts on the highest-yield areas will be your ticket to job search success. Here are some ways to set up a job search plan.

- **Appoint a job search "buddy."**
This person will be someone you report to on a weekly basis. This person will hold you accountable and be your "cheerleader" at the same time. NOTE: Make sure that this person is someone who is a friend, mentor or colleague. Don't rely on someone in your household… this could be a potential sticky wicket with family relationships if you somehow fall off the bandwagon and could lead to some very thorny arguments!

- **Number of articles to be read weekly.**
When you are unemployed or out of work, it is easy to feel that you are getting left behind on industry trends and issues. It's amazing that when you have a clear command of what's going on in the world, how incredibly easy it is to find opportunities to talk about what you've read or learned.

- **Number of networking events to attend weekly.**
Shy? Get over it. The job searching ocean is full of sharks right now, and you need to be one of them. That means getting out of the house, and getting out to networking events.

- **Number of educational events to go to monthly.**
When you are not working, again, there is the fear that you are out of the loop and losing ground to competitors. But smart job searchers realize that there is a huge opportunity to be gained during this time: take classes. This could be a great way to help catapult you into a new career, enhance your professional credentials, or hone your skills.

- **Number of volunteer hours per month.**
Volunteering can provide exceptional opportunities to network, learn new skills, become a known quantity within an organization and even find out about industry or company job openings before they are even posted. Plus, you'll feel good while doing it!

- **Number of member organizations to belong to.**
If you have a target industry, chances are that there is some kind of related trade association or membership organization that you could join. The benefit of these organizations is that your involvement can add gravitas to your credentials.

- **Number of informational interviews per week.**
Part of the "getting out of the house" aspect of this job search plan is to meet people… one-on-one in informational interviews. The best part about informational interviews is that if you treat the person right who took the time to meet with you, they can become a great internal champion for you. *Always* thank interviewees for their time by mailing a hand-written note.

- **Number of friends to talk to per week.**
Who do friends know? People. Employed people. Don't be afraid to reach out to your entire network. The key is to tap into your social circle and "refresh" your connections on a regular basis.

- **Follow up on sent applications.**

One of the biggest failures of job seekers is that they are constantly looking forward for the next job opening to apply for that they don't go back and follow up on the positions for which they've already applied. Sometimes, the position opening didn't turn out to be the right fit for your skills. But if you treat the hiring manager, recruiter, or the human resource representative right, you could impress them in a very good way. That could put you on the "A" list for other jobs that come open.

All of these activities probably seems like a whole lot of work, but the aim is to provide structure, stability and goals to you in a time where there is a lot of chaos, unclear objectives and confusion. By structuring yourself and your time while unemployed, this will give you the sense of purpose you need and also a boost to feeling productive.

Example job search spreadsheet:

Company	Position opening	Contact Phone	Contact Email	Sent appl. On:	Post Interview Thank you

Proactive Networking

In the advertising world, the axiom of a minimum of 5 "hits" before a message begins to stick is pretty accurate. Networking can never be considered complete with only one interaction. It does take several impressions/exposure incidents before someone really gets to know you and have a sense of who you are and what you might offer.

Proactive career managers don't fall into the "ice breaker" ship syndrome... which is where people make one networking contact akin to a ship breaking through the ice, only to let that ice freeze over behind them.

It is up to you to keep the newly forged lane behind you open – and that means making new contacts while making sure you stay busy refreshing those connections that you have already made.

Being an effective networker means staying in touch with your network of contacts, and refreshing those connections on a regular, consistent process.

Here are some ways you can achieve an active, engaged group of people with whom you have meaningful connections.

- **Send notes to them on special occasions (i.e. birthday).**
Facebook is great this way as it automatically lets users know when people in their network have a birthday. Seeing a note from you is another way to stay on their radar screen, and reinforces that connection.

- **Forwarding an article where the contact was featured.**
It's always a pleasant surprise to get an email or snail mail message from someone who saw you featured in an article as a way to flatter them tastefully.

- **Suggesting coffee or other social get-togethers on a monthly, quarterly, or annual basis.**
This is a great way to keep up-to-date with what is going on in your contact's life, and also gives you the opportunity to provide a quick snapshot of what you've been up to as well.

- **Send an article or news item that would be of interest to them.**
Forwarding information that you think your contact might want to know can be viewed as a thoughtful gesture. "Saw this and thought you

might be interested" is a great way to let them know that you are keeping them top-of-mind, and likely, as a result, they will do the same.

- **Involve or engage contacts in your work as appropriate.**
Are you working at a non-profit association that needs new committee or board members? One of the fastest ways to build affinity to the organization you are working for and to you as well for providing the opportunity is to make a direct ask for them to participate. Most people are thrilled to be considered, and this can also bolster their high opinion of you.

- **Be a "connector."**
One of my friends is someone that I rather jokingly (but in all seriousness) refer to as "The Grapevine" – she is a selfless connector who always listens to people and takes conversations a step further by being a resource who can identify opportunities to people, or by connecting like-minded people. Because she is always in motion by retaining information about people and needs, she has become one of the strongest networkers I know and a superior role model.

To this point, we tend to remember and stay in touch with those who have helped us in some way. In turn, we are more likely to return the favor should they need our help in the future.

- **Actively seek out leadership roles.**
By volunteering on a regular basis on committees or in groups that serve a specific purpose, you end up becoming a vital part of a project that has deliverables. The people you work with on those committees are your team members. You start out with virtually no knowledge of the others at the beginning, but by the end of the project, you have rapport and likely new friendships as a result of this shared experience. You'll also be fostering a reputation as a "doer" and now have a cadre of people who can speak to your character, leadership, and job skill expertise, too!

- **Follow up on new contacts... IMMEDIATELY.**

Unfortunately, many people think attending a meeting, collecting business cards, then coming home and shoving those cards into a desk drawer equals networking. WRONG! Networking is actually a life-long process that either succeeds or fails immediately after you connect with that person. Follow up with 24 hours with a follow up note or email: "It was great meeting you at _____, and I would love to learn more about _____. When would be a good time to sit down for coffee to chat?" is an easy and effective follow up technique.

Exercise caution about dismissing someone that you may have met just because they were not immediately helpful. Time and time again, I have found that opportunities come from the least expected places, and are not things you could have ever anticipated at the time of the initial meeting. If you nurture your network right, you are creating an opportunity pipeline not just for now, but also for the future. Follow up with everyone you meet, and if you play your cards right, it could lead to ideas and options you had not considered previously.

- **Never give up.**

Sometimes, people don't respond because either they didn't get your message, are otherwise occupied with more pressing deadlines, a spam filter caught your note, or any number of other reasons. But you can't give up and take non-responses personally if you are proactively networking towards a specific goal. Try a different method on another day, and you might be rewarded... but, of course, know the fine line between being politely persistent and being perceived as the dreaded "stalker!"

STAYING MOTIVATED DURING A JOB SEARCH

There's nothing like putting yourself out there only to be rejected... which all comes as part of the territory during a job search. You can and WILL be excluded... a lot. The odds are simply against you when applying for only one job and ending up being the final candidate selected.

Of course, turndowns are always deflating... and it is easy to end up feeling sad, lonely, and dejected. "No one wants me" is a common thought when job seekers get this down in the dumps.

As the sole captain of your job search ship, you will need to make sure to keep yourself motivated and positive... no matter what. Here are some tips to keep yourself moving.

- **Pamper yourself.**

Do something that you enjoy and makes you feel happy. This is a little indulgence to remind yourself that you are awesome. Because you are!

- **Take a break.**

You need to take a break from the job of finding a job... so make sure you mindfully plan and prepare for time off. This can mean taking a short vacation or making sure that weekends are free to do fun activities so you can take some pressure off of yourself.

- **Volunteer.**

This activity has already been discussed as a positive way to add to skills and relevant experience, but volunteering also does something else: It boosts your endorphin levels which are the "feel good" hormones. This could be just the boost you need to take the focus off yourself and onto someone less fortunate.

- **Schedule face-time with your cheerleaders.**

Getting together with your mentors and advocates will do wonders for you. They can provide the positive feedback and support you crave during this tough time. As your sounding board, these supporters can also provide suggestions for improvement and fresh ideas to help you keep on the "up" side of a job search.

- **Review your job search diary to see your progress.**
Being organized in your job search will also help you be able to see how effective you are and feel forward momentum. Look at how many contacts you made over a week, month, and year. Eventually, you will snare something in the giant web that you are weaving, and by keeping steady notes of your progress, you'll feel better about the fact that you have been making progress.

- **Re-invent yourself.**
Seeking professional résumé writing assistance or career coaching can help you give a refreshing boost to your job search. Résumé clients that I have worked with have expressed feelings of being absolutely reborn with a new document – it is like a new lease on life and they feel completely re-energized and excited about the job search process as a result. This is a great way to get motivated by rebooting your efforts with a totally new perspective.

INNOVATIVE JOB SEARCH IDEAS

Most of us know that in order to apply for a job, there's a sort of formula to the entire process: Company posts job, people network their way into job, applications are sent in, applications are screened, then serious candidates are called in for one or multiple rounds of interviews, and then a final selection is made.

Because this formula is so established, there's a certain routine to it. But what makes headlines are people who disrupt that routine with innovative ideas that work outside of "business as usual."

Here are some ideas to get your thoughts flowing about what you might be able to do to shift the job search paradigm.

- **Throw a job search "shower" or "Pink Slip Party".**

In the December 2009 issue of *Marie Claire* magazine, an article show-cased a job search shower which is much along the lines of a bridal shower. But instead of party favors, the person throwing the shower hosts drinks and has a "job registry" of specific target positions or employers, and asks attendees to come to the shower with either leads, contacts, or help in any other job search arena. This and Pink Slip Parties are great ways to get your friends engaged in your job search.

- **"Confidential" mailers.**

As we now almost exclusively use electronic means of communication, "snail mail" is quickly getting overlooked as a way to stand out. Most of us can barely remember the last time we actually got a hand-written note in the mail, so sending your application over in a priority envelope marked "confidential" gets immediate attention.

- **Vanity "Googling."**

The *Huffington Post* reported in May 2010 that copywriter Alec Brownstein bought up Google AdWords for five top advertising executives... knowing that it is human nature to check out their own search results. He paid $6 (about $.10 per click) to get the top search result for each person which was titled, "Hey, (name of executive)" which included a message to the executive. Brownstein got interviews with four of the five executives, and job offers from two.

- **Offer financial incentive for job leads converting to an offer.**

Some job seekers are taking it to the extreme to motivate their net-works. One person I know was offering a $1,500 payday to the person in their contacts who referred the one lead that turned into a bonafide job offer. Actually, this is pretty smart... considering it could take sev-eral months to find a similar offer on your own, this could cut your job search shorter, and you could make up this expense the first month of your new job with the new salary.

- **Send a gift card for coffee to target person.**
Some job seekers have sent Starbucks gift cards to hiring managers or key contacts at target companies. However, use good judgment by not trying to "suck up" to the actual people who influence final candidate decisions for job openings. The gift card usually provokes some kind of response from the recipient – it is unusual, and invites a conversation over coffee bought by the card.

- **Start a Twitter campaign.**
In addition to boosting your visibility over social media, a campaign on Twitter can be effective in getting noticed. You can re-tweet the company's posts, send a message with an article post attached that is of interest to the company, answer/ask questions relevant to the company's field, and thank/acknowledge any replies you do get. Create a landing page to send people to if they are interested in learning more about you, and even better, put that URL directly into your Twitter profile so it is there 24/7!

- **Join an HR membership group.**
Sun-tzu said: "Keep your friends close; keep your enemies closer" so if you journey to the "belly of the beast" by attending or joining a HR group that is in your field, you might gain a better chance to get to know the key players and build rapport with them. This is a bit of a long-shot, but could prove helpful in the long-term by being able to mix directly with those contacts.

- **Write a letter to the company president.**
Some job seekers go the very direct route and send a letter of interest to the company president, who, of course, is always busy and hands off the letter to one of their underlings. But that person could be above the hiring manager for the position that you are targeting, so there could be a trickle-down effect of the senior manager directing the person who is your boss to give you a call to learn more!

- **Send a package with a new shoe enclosed letting them know you want to "get a foot in door."**

A cute way to get someone's attention, you should be aware that sometimes this can backfire if they don't "get" it!

- **Get some personalized fortune cookies made.**

Not only are you delivering a treat, but the message inside can read something along the lines of "Your company fortunes are about to become richer by hiring _____."

- **Sending a jigsaw puzzle piece attached to your résumé.**

Include the message with the puzzle piece: "Here's the missing piece to your team."

- **Become a member.**

For some non-profit or trade organizations, being a member in good standing can and does make a difference. One job seeker's experience: "One time I was interviewing with AAA for a position, and at the moment that I was asked to present my membership card (and I didn't have one), I knew I had lost the job."

- **Create an employer-specific YouTube video appeal.**

Social media can allow us to be more fun and creative in our approaches, but be very careful about this tactic. There are countless hapless people who created what they thought were compelling "Hire me" videos for employers and are now laughingstocks on the Internet. If you aren't hiring a professional production company to put something together, you might want to re-think whether you want to potentially become a living legend online… in a bad sense.

- **Gift certificate to employer of your services.**

Some job seekers have started offering these as a "trial period" of their services, but in a way, some human resource professionals might interpret this as complete desperation. You should always have some sense of the value of what you offer so if you decide to go this route, make sure you put a valuation (based on a competitive salary) of your services.

- **Make job search T-shirts/placards.**

These can be a novel approach but again, the placement has to be spot-on or it will come across flat. One person even took out an outdoor billboard display across from the office where he wanted to work... that may have come across as overkill!

These are just a few of the many creative ideas out there for making your job search stand out in a novel way. But most experts are unanimous that job seekers, no matter how inventive or creative their approach may be, still need to deliver on the résumé and cover letter content. You may have the ability to catch the attention of the target audience, but you still need to deliver the goods that match employer needs.

ON THE JOB #FAIL: GAME OVER?

Before we get too deep into job searching, there's one thing that needs to be addressed... because it is going to come up and you need to deal with it.

So let's talk turkey about a very painful topic: Failure.

Eeeek! Run for the hills!

In fact, the topic was so uncomfortable that when I posted a request online asking for some help writing about on-the-job failures, do you know what I got?

Absolute radio silence.

Riiiiiight… so I guess that means that everyone out there is all absolutely flawless and without fault?

Probably not. However, this response pretty much confirmed my suspicions and the very reason for addressing this issue in the first place: Everyone is too scared to talk about their job failures. In fact, most of us have probably have repressed our slip-ups, instead of embracing them.

So why exactly does job failure hurt so much, and why are we so darned scared of it?

Business and quality management guru Philip Crosby once said: "Very few of the great leaders ever get through their careers without failing, sometimes dramatically."

Now we know that even the "big dogs" have failed, but the sting remains: How can failure impact our own lives and/or careers? What if I really screwed up at work, as in a major boo-boo? What about (gulp)…. me?

In search of the answers, I went to an unusual source: Jason Zasky, editor of *Failure* magazine. Yes, you read that correctly. His magazine is all about failure.

"Failure is more interesting than success," was Zasky's response when I called him to talk about this topic. "And even more importantly, it's a universal experience."

Aw c'mon everyone, time to be honest. We all mess up at some point in our careers, including those squirming, gut-wrenching, and totally anguishing #EPICFAILS.

I'll even admit my "biggie": when I was in my early 20's, I utterly derailed a tradeshow I had planned by neglecting the marketing. OOP-sie… It was my first big project, and while I executed the event planning/executing flawlessly, the one small detail of working with the marketing person didn't even cross my mind (are you cringing yet?). End result: Gorgeous tradeshow with 100% booth sell-out. Attendance: not so much.

Ouch. Talk about a lot of steamed (politely speaking) exhibitors... I got an earful but was able to learn from the experience... and never made the same mistake again!

Zasky said that there are three things that prevent the majority of us from properly addressing reasons as to why we have failed at some point in our jobs.

"Failure itself is embarrassing, humbling, and hard to overcome... which then leads to non-action. You've got to confront things head-on, learn from them, and then move on. And never give up."

So really, it's what we *do* with those failures that really matters?

You betcha.

Failure can keep you from reaching your potential if you let it. While it can be darned uncomfortable when you address it directly, failure can be one of the most compelling learning experiences... that is, if you are willing to embrace it.

In short, you've absolutely got to get cozy with your failure in order to win the ultimate take-away: lessons learned.

Today, people are more willing to accept failure and to learn from it. You can see this acceptance dramatically divided along generational lines these days, according to Zasky.

While people who are in their 20s-30s today ricochet through failures like a pinball between bumpers, workers born in the Depression-era simply don't accept the term "failure." It wasn't an option offered during their upbringing, and this generation avoids it at all costs.

But failure *is* an option today.

In fact, many companies are now rewarding employees for calculated risk-taking... sometimes the endgame has become all about rewarding the risk-taking/lessons learned from failures that can lead to those coveted "homeruns."

What can you learn from this?

Getting too wrapped up in failure is what can hurt your career. Don't let the very fear of failure itself rule you.

Finally willing to admit a few career miscues? Take the following empowering steps to confront failure.

- **Admit it. It hurts, but it's yours and yours alone.**
Try not to externalize blame to everyone else.

- **Do an objective, realistic autopsy of the failure.**
What parts did you fall down on, and what were some contributing factors that you had no control over?

- **Discover the hidden "nugget."**
How can you either improve what you do, or avoid making the same mistakes?

- **Don't let it consume you.**
You need to be able to accept the failure and move on.

You can and will get over failure. In hindsight, it can be a powerful experience that no one can teach you. Turning around and facing it can have positive far-reaching impacts on your career.

Remember, failure doesn't have to be "GAME OVER" for your career... unless you let it.

5

Put on the Lights! It's Showtime!

Preparing for Interviews Impacts Your Career Direction

"All things are difficult before they are easy."
- Thomas Fuller

Many times, we don't consciously think about what we need to do to prepare for an interview until we get the call that an employer wants to talk to us about a job opening. Then all hell breaks loose. It's a mad scramble to pull together documents and read up on a company to be as up-to-speed as possible before heading in.

Interviews are undoubtedly one of the most difficult steps in the entire job search process.

But as a person who actively manages your career, your goal is to keep those target companies within your sights for much longer time than a explicit job posting period.

Being conscious of which specific companies would be desirable places to work can help you become ingrained in their culture, values, needs, challenges, and opportunities far in advance of target job opening.

The idea is that by the time you actually sit down with the employer, you are ready to have an engaging, informed conversation. You won't be thinking about the fact that you want the job. You'll be more interested in a give-and-take discussion that is really a business meeting. And that's exactly how well-prepared career managers see interviews taking place.

Something to consider: Do you think that CEOs are sitting there in the interview, wringing their hands and worrying what the other people are thinking about them? ("Will they like me?" "Did I answer that question correctly?") No. The confident CEO is interested in a discussion to find out if there is a match between what the company needs, and what they offer to meet that need. Simply put, they are interested in <u>learning</u> more about the job. You should be, too!

Of all times in the entire job search process, the interview should be the point where you are the most excited, versus being nervous and letting the pressure build.

You and only you are in charge of your career destiny, and you need to reshape your thinking about interviews. It is time to see them as a positive conversation where you get to demonstrate your interest and enthusiasm in the opening, and skillfully use the discussion to highlight your ability to solve their needs.

Learning to relax and enjoy the opportunity to have a dialogue about this job opportunity is what we all hope for… so spend your energy on thinking about how awesome it is that you have been selected for a coveted interview!

The reason why most people have a difficult time with interviews is that they end up psyching themselves out and <u>making the outcome the purpose of the conversation</u>, rather than actually having the discussion itself about the job.

Your goal is to overcome those fears and re-engineer how you see the interview into an opportunity to talk to the decision makers about something you are very excited about!

INTERVIEW PREPARATION

It is stunning to see how many people arrive at an interview ill-prepared and disorganized, which immediately makes the wrong impression. Preparation is key.

This is just the first step. Being completely prepared to head off to an interview requires a checklist.

- **Bring the full contact information of the interviewer.**
One time in a million, an accident can happen to you enroute to an interview. If you can do so (safely), call the interviewer as a courtesy to let them know that you had a flat tire, etc. just so you don't leave them hanging. Simply not showing up is a deal- and career-killer.

- **Arrive early.**

Use Mapquest or another mapping feature to get a precise location on your interview destination. Budget plenty of time for traffic tie-ups. Bring enough change for parking meters if you need to use one. I always suggest arriving 15-20 minutes early to your parking spot, and spend five minutes "staging" yourself before arriving ten minutes prior to your interview.

- **Bring key materials.**

The résumé you submitted to the company, your cover letter, a list of references, list of questions you want to ask, notepad/portfolio, two pens, copy of the job description, a business card (if you have one), relevant work samples, and any background research you've been able to dig up.

- **TURN OFF YOUR PHONE!**

It is always an expectation that you should have turned off your phone, but we are all human and forget from time to time before going into an important appointment. But nothing else puts an interviewer's teeth on edge than a candidate's phone going off in the middle of the interview… unless you actually end up taking the call. (Don't!)

- **No food, drink, or gum.**

Eat or drink something before or after the interview, but never during. (Yes, I have actually seen someone bring a sandwich to an interview… we were all aghast!) This boycott includes not bringing a soda drink to the waiting room. If you are offered water, you can accept; some people get so nervous that they get dry mouth during interviews and need a drink of water. If the employer offers, it is fine to accept this. But be careful about fidgeting with the glass on the table during the interview. And if you have bad breath, chew a mint on the way to the interview. (And don't plan on indulging on the garlic-heavy spaghetti dinner the night before!)

- **Write down the names of your interviewer(s).**

You'll need that information to refer to them later during the interview (nothing communicates confidence more than using that person's name when addressing them), and also for your follow-up thank you note either mailed or emailed to EACH interviewer.

Being calm, focused, and prepared can play a huge role in how you portray yourself walking into the interview. Do you want to arrive flustered, running late, and disorganized? Or be cool and collected, with no anxiety sitting on your coattails?

Phone/Video Interviews

Every job seeker should be prepared for a potential phone or video interview. If you don't have a webcam for your computer, you can head to a local electronics store and usually find a good quality one under $30. Newer smart phones are also equipped with video cameras as well, but for a more stable shot, the computer-based ones are best.

Prepping for a phone or video interview is much different than going to a company. In addition to getting all of your ducks in row in terms of reviewing questions and researching the business, you also have to think in terms of getting your setting ready as well.

Top things you need to think about when you are in this type of interview setting in order to put your best foot forward:

- **Find a quiet place.**

Hopefully, your home office or computer is set up in an area where you can close the door and windows to remove external sounds penetrating the room like sirens, traffic, or any other extraneous noise. You want all audio coming from your end to only be the sound of your voice, nothing else.

- **Tell other people in household you are not to be disturbed.**

This includes intrusions, questions, background noise (like televisions), creaky floors, operation of noisy machines (dishwashers), and anything else that might serve as a disruption.

- **Secure childcare.**

Children don't understand that their parents are not to be disturbed and can interrupt interviews. Having a crying child in the background or one demanding attention during an interview is highly disruptive to the conversational dynamic you are trying to build with the interviewers.

Try to find someone who can watch children during your meeting... plan on at least 2 hours – about 40 minutes for the interview and a half and hour on each end of the interview so you can prep beforehand without distractions and have some time to review how you did afterwards.

- **Moving pets out of earshot.**

Like children, animals don't understand that you don't wish to be interrupted, and can cause quite a commotion. Putting pets outside or in another room where they won't get stirred up is a smart idea, and will help you stay focused on the conversation. Don't forget that Fluffy the cat might be in the habit of jumping on your keyboard (and in visual range of your webcam) so keeping the door shut is a good idea, too.

- **Turn off all potential distractions.**

If you are in your home office, turn off all email programs and social media notices so you aren't distracted by constant pinging of message notifications. Turn off your cell phone if you are on a landline or on a video call... this goes for faxes as well. The only thing you should be paying attention to is the phone or the video camera, nothing else.

- **Dress the same you would for an in-person interview.**

Regardless of the fact that you might be having a phone call, you should absolutely dress up like you were walking right into the prospective employer's office. How you look and feel about how you look impacts your demeanor and ultimately, how you come across in the interview.

- **Do set "dressing."**

Preparing for a video call is like setting up for a television show. In the small window that the camera provides into your space, employers can and will be looking at everything else in the picture in addition to you. Creating a professional look can be as simple as turning your camera towards a blank wall with you sitting in front of it, but you do want to make sure you feel comfortable in the setting as well.

Remove anything that might be unseemly, unprofessional, or disturbing in the background. Conduct a test run to make sure the lighting is complimentary; you certainly don't want to look like a mug shot or be half-bathed in shadows…or at the very worst: a deer caught in headlights!

Thinking about all of these factors will help you better prepare for this type of interview and be more comfortable.

WHO'S DRIVING THE INTERVIEW BUS?

So, who is exactly in control during the actual interview? Did you guess the employer?

Wrong.

You BOTH are in control.

Most job applicants mentally hand over all the power in a job search to the prospective employer, being that they (the employer) have something that the candidate wants (the job). It's easy to think that the target company is the sole decision maker as to whether they hire that person or not.

This is a dangerous attitude to take, because in essence, you are effectively handing over the power of the situation to someone else, when in fact, you equally hold the reins.

Remember, the employer also has a need and is looking for the best way to fill that need in the most expedient manner possible.

If you have carefully managed your career, are confident in your abilities and what it is that you offer to the employer, you also have control in the interview room just as much as the employer. Flip the dynamics around, and suddenly you are the industry subject matter expert who is top in your field, and what you offer is exactly what the employer is seeking (perhaps even desperately so).

Preparing for interviews truly boils down to three things: Subject matter expertise, knowledge of the position/company, and enthusiasm/confidence. If you have these three pieces, you have a great start to what promises to be a successful discussion. You'll be so relaxed and confident about those three areas that the rest will fall into place.

Achieving those three critical benchmarks requires preparation, and lots of it. Knowledge is power, and getting yourself prepared is not something that happens overnight. As soon as you find out that you have been selected to be interviewed, you need to begin intensive study to learn as much as you can about the company.

Learning about the overall corporate culture, personalities you'll be working with, the "deeper" job description that insiders can provide, and what kinds of assets and liabilities the company has will be pivotal to your preparing the right responses to interview questions.

Author Susan Britton Whitcomb, mentioned previously in this book, also has another great book, *Interview Magic,* which walks through the main types of interviewing techniques, and provides a great hands-on guide on how to work through the interview preparation process as well as how to handle responding to questions.

But key to any interview success, you should be aware of the career drivers that can impact how the interviewers perceive you and influence whether they want to make you their hiring choice.

- **Authenticity.**
Be yourself... "fake it 'til you make it" simply doesn't fly in today's economy. Employers are getting more sophisticated and able to sniff out smoke screens from lesser qualified applicants trying to puff themselves up to something that they aren't. Focus on being the best you that you can be in the interview, but don't be a chameleon and change your stripes so much that you can't recognize yourself from one job interview to the next.

By being true to your authentic self, you'll connect better with those who are interviewing you, and you won't have to worry about covering your tracks later in case you answered something differently that doesn't really jive with your true core.

- **Enthusiasm.**
Being fired up about a job truly resonates with interviewers and can prove to be a strong influence on the final decision makers. This is the "gut" instinct that is a reinforcement of the employer's choice in you as their final candidate. And if you aren't as fired up about the job by the time you hit the interview, this could give interviewers pause.

- **Engagement.**

Being interested in the company, people, and the position and how they all interact together comes across as engaged, versus just passing interest in a simple job opening. Employers want you to like their company and the job opening as much as they want to like you. Showing energy, excitement, and an interest in a dialogue is a fabulous way to show active involvement and interest during the interview process.

- **Beware of your speaking cadence.**

When we get nervous, we tend to speed up how fast we are talking. Remember to slow it down, breathe, and use "pregnant pauses" to break up your responses.

Additionally, some people's voices go up a few notches in terms of pitch which can convey discomfort or distress to the intended audience. Make sure you are conscious about how you are talking just as much as how you are saying it.

Another thing to pay attention to is avoid the use of hedgers like "um" or "ah" while you are talking. They can become distracting to your audience and make you sound disorganized. The more succinctly and concisely you can directly answer questions, the more focused and sharp you'll appear.

- **Project confidence.**

The most confident people are the ones who make even eye contact and also use people's names in the interview when addressing them. Example: "Well, Jane, that is a very good question – I am more than happy to answer it." The best interviewees don't fidget and keep their eyes focused on the interviewer(s) rather than flitting around the room or out the window.

Don't slouch – when you start rolling your shoulders inward, you are physically signaling to others that you are closing yourself off. Sit up straight, square your shoulders and keep your body language open to send a subconscious note to interviewers that you are confident.

Another way to exude confidence is to project well. Be careful about being soft-spoken because you might be considered too timid or not assertive enough to do the job. You don't have to shout, but practice projecting in a clear voice at an easily heard volume.

- **Stuck in an answer? Run towards it, not away from it.**
Sometimes, you'll get that one question that absolutely stumps you. It may mean that you simply don't have the answer. Don't be afraid of it… instead, address it directly instead of making a dodge, then redirect back to the discussion.

Example: "Well, Jane, I don't actually have that skill, but that is one of the reasons why I would like to work here because this would be a great opportunity to learn it from one of the industry experts. Can you tell me a little more about how this skill would be used in this position or company?"

- **Non-verbal body language.**
Be focused on how you hold your hands, what kind of eye contact you make, and how you might be clearing your throat. Most information that we gather about someone else comes from non-verbal communication, and if you are sending out signals to the interviewer that you are not comfortable or highly nervous, this can overpower what you actually say in the answers that you give.

- **Expertise/job knowledge.**
If you have made it to the interview stage, an employer believes that you have enough job expertise in the area for which they are hiring that they want to talk to you. Many times, the people doing the hiring don't have the precise knowledge of all the ins and outs that the position actually

requires, and are depending on you to be able to handle those minutia as part of your competency in that field.

- ### Know the company inside and out.

Have you ever been asked this question point-blank in an interview: "What do you know about our company and why do you think we should hire you?

A great trick to really knock their socks off? Create a binder on the company. Go to the office supply store and get one of those 3-ring binders with clear sleeves on the outside. Create a title page that you slip in that includes the company's logo where you are interviewing so it is noticeable on the spine as well as main cover.

When you walk in, the interviewers are immediately going to start wondering how and why you have a binder on their company. It's a great conversation ice-breaker, and it piques their interest as well. Once you explain, it further underscores how resourceful you are! Inside, you will have key pages from the company website as well as relevant articles pertaining to the interview that you can make notes on for reference.

- ### Be pre-emptive to take the pressure off.

The most awkward and uncomfortable part of the interview is actually getting escorted in and then starting the discussion. You can completely start shaping the discussion in several ways before the interview even begins.

I always suggest, once the interviewer points you to the seat where you will be sitting, to point at the chair and say, "Oh, is this the hot seat?? I hope you have it warmed up… I'm rarin' to go!" This immediately conveys confidence, gentle humor, and enthusiasm all at once.

Another trick to take the pressure off is to actually slide into the driver's seat. One way to do this is by "inserting" a question or statement that gets the conversation going but it is on your terms.

Example: (as the interviewer guides you to the interview area) "Gosh, I cannot tell you how excited I am about this interview. When I was reading an article in _____, I started wondering about _____.... what can you tell me about this?" It is a simple technique but you are getting them talking first and this can also provide you valuable "pre-info" to the interview that can help steer how you develop your responses to their questions.

- **Don't ramble.**

Most of us have heard of the popular culture term "TMI" which means "too much information" – you'd be surprised how many people continue on and provide irrelevant information in the interview that ends up getting painted into a corner. Stick only to the facts that are relevant to the question.

- **Respect yourself, just as you respect the employer.**

If the person or people interviewing you aren't showing you the same amount of respect that you'd expect, write an "X" against the employer. Just like you, the employer's representatives should be on their best behavior during the interview. Think of this as the "courtship" phase when everything should be all "go" and not any "no!" Don't like how they are treating you? It's a sure sign that worse things are yet to come if you do get the job.

- **Test for chemistry.**

Just as there are good bosses out there, there are also bad bosses. We've seen them. Control freaks, neurotic messes, people with anger issues... they are all out there. The question is: Are they sitting in front of you in an interview?

REAL-WORLD EXAMPLE

I was once interviewing at a large corporation where the HR person (!!!) told me that the CEO that I was going to be directly reporting to had extreme anger issues and treated staff horribly. Then the HR person asked how I would handle that. At that point, I chose not to handle it. Who needs that lying on your doorstep every day? If it isn't a fit, walk away. You'll save yourself from ulcers, high blood pressure, and a miserable existence. Sure, it could be the job you've always wanted, but at what cost?

- **Watch the interview team for clues on team dynamics.**

If you are in a panel interview, or have successive follow-up interviews, examine how the team communicates. Is there camaraderie? Are they having fun? Or are they sour, droll, or beaten down? Clues to the team dynamic can also give you a heads up on the corporate culture.

I remember during one interview many years ago that there were several people on the panel who seemed rather combative. Fortunately, I had done my research and found out that the organization had been suffering from a lot of external politics, and the observation of these folks in the interview verified this revelation which came from an inside source. I weighed everything after the interview, and that was the determining factor of why I chose not to accept the position. Again, if they were fighting in the interview, what kind of toxic work environment would I be getting myself into?

- **ALWAYS ask questions.**

Let me put it this way: if you don't ask questions, this absolutely reflects very poorly on you. Questions are your most valuable tool to address any "blanks" you might have about the company and/or position. They can also be a measurement instrument on how you are answering their questions.

You should always have a list of at least 10 predetermined questions that you want to ask during the interview, or at the very end when directed. And if the interview is wrapping up and they still haven't offered you the opportunity to ask any questions, this is a good time to pipe in and say, "I am so excited about this position, and I was wondering if I could ask you a few questions to add to my understanding of what we have already discussed?"

In all likelihood, you won't use all of the questions you brought as many are answered during the course of the discussion.

But you should have a strong mix of things to ask including job-specific queries as well as company-specific ones.

- **Do a "temperature check" at the end of the interview.**

This is a critical juncture. Usually employers will close the interview and say thank you, etc. But once you walk out of that room, the chances of you getting feedback on how you actually performed falls to practically zero.

Proactive, career-management related questions to ask in an interview:

Based on what you've seen today, do you have any questions or concerns about my ability to do the job?

What kinds of professional development opportunities doe this company offer?

What are the biggest challenges that your company has faced in the past 5 years?

What are the biggest opportunities that you see in the next year for the company?

What are three things that I need to know in order to hit the ground running?

What are the top priorities in the next few months for this position?

What happened to the previous person who held this job?

How would you describe your management style?

Could you describe the attributes and expertise for what you would consider the ideal candidate for this position?

Can you describe the organizational structure?

They've put you on the spot, so it's time to be assertive and put them on the spot as well. This is your one and only opportunity to find out how you did.

Ask, "Based on our discussion today, do you have any concerns about my ability to perform this position?" By posing this question, you are holding them accountable for their ultimate hiring decision… you'll find out right away how you rate in the interviewer's estimation, and have a good understanding as to why you were or were not chosen for the position. This tactic can also enable you to address any outstanding issues or concerns that they might have about your ability to do the job.

Too many times, most of us walk away without any kind of closure of our performance. We may sort of know, but don't really have a sense of what the employer is thinking. The only way you can improve your interviewing skills is by learning, and by asking this question, you are creating a learning opportunity to empower yourself to do better in future interviews.

Steve Levy, a New York City-based technical recruiter always likes candidates to ask these questions:

"Why would the very best person want this job?"

"Why would the very best person want to work for this manager?"

"Let's look out one year from now – what did this person accomplish to be considered 'wildly successful' by the manager and the company?"

According to Levy, when candidates pose these questions, it demonstrates to the interviewer that you are performance-oriented rather than task-oriented. And that's what separates the "wheat from the chaff" in his mind.

"If the recruiter comes back and asks why you need to know these things, you need to tell them that you believe work is about solving problems, and in order for you to make a conscientious and informed decision about the opportunity, you need to know about the real job that is beyond the job description," adds Levy.

In his experience, by asking those questions, you'll get one of two responses…

"Wow – no one has ever asked me such great questions! I don't know the answers but I'll get them for you. Thank YOU!"

Or…

"You're such a pain; I'd rather work with someone who genuflects in my presence and doesn't ask such questions."

Well, not really, but there are some recruiters who have the wrong attitude. Unfortunately, you won't be able to change that perspective if you run into that wall. This can be very disappointing, especially if this is a position that you are very excited about.

Be aware, though, that going around recruiters and directly to an employer is usually not a good idea because the company hired the recruiter in the first place so they wouldn't have to handle the vetting process.

In fact, this could result in you getting blacklisted, which can be a bad thing especially if the recruiter is dominant in your particular field.

Who's on First? ABCs of Who Is Interviewing You

Most people don't realize that there is actually a difference between all the different types of interviewers. Take a moment to see the difference:

Recruiter: Acts as a third party broker on behalf of client companies and recruits talent on behalf of customer; makes recommendations on candidate choices that influences client company hiring decisions.

Headhunter: Similar to recruiter but tracks executive-level candidates and their work histories on a longer-term basis to be able to quickly make recommendations to company clients.

Hiring Manager: The person at a company who will make the final decision over the hire and your likely new supervisor.

Human Resources: The person who ensures all legal aspects of the hiring process are followed and acts as an initial screener. Can also make hiring decisions.

PERSONAL ATTENTION TO GROOMING

Interview situations can be a little tricky in terms of what to wear, but you should always opt on the side of conservative, formal attire unless told otherwise. Human beings are very visual creatures, and it is widely accepted that within the first 6 seconds of meeting you, employers have already made some assumptions about you, and how you present yourself will make the lasting impression for which you will be remembered.

The hardest part for students and new graduates when it comes to the interview process is that they are used to clothes defining themselves within their own peer groups, and now all of a sudden, they are expected to conform to someone else's standard. It is a foreign and disorienting feeling.

But considering you have already spent hours of time preparing your résumé and cover letter, applying for the job, then even more time in the interview preparation process, doesn't it seem pretty dumb to blow all that hard work within those first few moments when the employer finally meets you?

Think this doesn't happen?

Think again.

In one of my former jobs, I worked with a lot of employers who were interested in hiring youth entering the work force. Over 80% of the companies I worked with told me that they would instantly hire "the first best-dressed kid" before even looking at their résumé. Hard to believe, but that does show you how much appearance matters. In many cases, the employer is thinking about how you will represent them to their customers.

REAL-WORLD EXAMPLE
I remember one time where a student at a rural high school was having trouble getting employed, despite the fact that he had an accomplished résumé and skill set.

As it turned out, he had a mohawk haircut, and the jobs that he was applying for were as a server at one of the town's handful of cafés. No one would hire him because the owners were afraid he would scare away customers. This took place in a small, economically depressed logging town on a highway which brought tourists through to the beach… these transient customers were the lifeblood of those businesses. The café owners could not afford to have a "scary-looking" server driving away business. The outcome: The student eventually cut his hair and was immediately offered a job.

The whole point here is that you can definitely decide how you want to express yourself on your time, but when you enter the workplace, the employer is hiring you as their representative. Their expectation is that you will act in their interests at all time, and are concerned about your ability to carry that off by projecting a professional image inline with that of the company.

The good news is that many companies let you wear what you want after you get the job, but when it comes to the first impression, there is no going back after it has been made.

Your best bet?

For men: clean shaven, no piercings or tattoos visible, dress shoes and socks, nice pants (either dress or casual dress), and a nice shirt as well as a belt. Depending on the company, a tie and sport coat might be appropriate. For more conservative companies and corporate settings, a two-piece suit and tie might be more proper for the interview.

Women: Non-revealing clothing with appropriate (knee-length or lower) hemlines, no visible piercings or tattoos, nice blouse, jacket, skirt or pants, and nice shoes. No open-toed shoes... save the flip-flops for summertime outings to the beach.

Both men and women should avoid showy jewelry, and use minimal or no perfumes or colognes.

Career-savvy professionals also use the interview process to collect information about the overall office culture and appropriate clothing cues.

Handling Terminations In An Interview

The most gut-wrenching words you never want to hear that seem like the end of the world: "You're fired" or "We are going to have to let you go."

Terminations happen; whether your fault or because someone decided to eliminate you for their own personal ambition or agenda.

But the end result is the same: Being fired from a job can taint your future prospects.

The biggest worry that previously terminated job seekers have when looking for work is whether someone else will give them a chance, despite this ding on their career record.

If this unfortunate situation has happened to you, be aware that before you even get to the interview table, you need to have an attitude adjustment about what that termination means.

You need to seize control of it, and own it. Don't let it own you.

Here are some tips to help you get past this difficult time in your career and overcome the pain of a termination.

- **Bury the negativity with positivity.**
Out of work right now? Try volunteering, and wow them with going above and beyond what is asked of you. The volunteer work can be listed in your employment history (be sure to indicate "Volunteer (job name)"). The good news? You've started to create a positive track record

of what you can capably deliver, and also redefined yourself in a better light. Plus, you'll feel better so the last (and most recent) thing in your career isn't negative, which is a powerful booster to your mental state during the job search.

- **Remove preconceptions.**

Act the part by dressing, acting, and speaking professionally in every single interaction that you have with an employer. Don't give them a reason to doubt your abilities.

- **Address the problems that led to your termination.**

If you did make a mistake big enough to warrant termination, you need to be willing to investigate those reasons. Do you have an anger problem? Are you lacking in a skill that resulted in a less-than-satisfactory performance? Be willing to examine the contributing causes, no matter how painful they seem at the time. Identifying, knowing, and then working to resolve the problems that led to this situation will help you better prepare for the future.

- **Accept blame where it is due… then let go of the rest.**

Even if your termination honestly had nothing to do with your job performance, you can't change the course of history. Whatever circumstances led to the termination were obviously beyond your control, and while it is okay to be upset and angry about the outcome, it is best to not stew about things… you can't change them and your energy is better served helping yourself towards the future, versus agonizing about the past.

- **Understand that you will need to explain your dismissal.**

Potential employers will find out anyway, so this is your one opportunity to answer the question before it is even asked and to influence the decision maker's opinion about you. Explain you ran into a difficult situation with your last employer and that trying to make them happy simply didn't work out, which is why you left. Bring up the point that you have good references from previous employers who can speak to your abilities and productivity.

Employers want to know under what circumstances you left, and if there was a problem, how you either learned from it or solved it... so it isn't a potential issue for the prospective company.

Redirect the unavoidable question and shape it into a positive statement that steers away from the emotions of leaving your previous employer. By doing this, you can deflect the attention away from the negative situation and stay focused on the current job opening at hand.

But never (EVER) launch into a negative tirade about a previous employer. In an interviewer's eyes, this is seen as a preview to what might happen, should they have to terminate you, and they certainly don't want people bad-mouthing their company or staff members.

Try to turn the negatives into positives... and redirect. The simplest formula for talking about terminations in interviews is as follows:

Acknowledge that you were terminated + What you learned (or positive outcomes) = how you are better suited now as a result to help the interviewer.

Example: "I was let go from my previous employer because I made some accounting errors. In retrospect, I did not have the opportunity to brush up on the new software program because we were so busy. Since then, however, I have completed additional bookkeeping and accounting classes to address those skill gaps, and feel confident that my up-to-date knowledge and drive to keep learning will be an asset to your organization's financial operations."

BIZARRO © 2009 DAN PIRARO. KING FEATURES SYNDICATE

The example shows how you admitted the situation (didn't run away from it), owned up to it (accountability), understood the problem, then took steps to rectify it to then render yourself more capable than before.

Tackling a termination head-on is not only honest, but also empowering. You are now in a position to avoid letting the fear of what happened in the past cloud your future.

THE MOST IMPORTANT THING TO REMEMBER ABOUT INTERVIEWING

No matter what, whether you are on the fence as to whether you want the job or not, you must never come across as being anything less than 100% excited about the job during the interview.

If you aren't completely fired up, you can count on the interviewers reading you like a book. Many times, they can actually see a candidate trying to decide whether they want a job or not right there during the actual interview. And at that point, it's game over. You can almost see their excitement evaporate from the room as well, and then the rest of the interview ends up being a painfully bad conversation.

Coming to this decision of not wanting the job might be the result of learning things about the company or the position that may change your mind. Something may happen in the interview which you might feel damage your chances for the position or you might observe some behavior that starts waving red flags. But you absolutely must maintain 10,000% excitement and engagement throughout the interview to keep the dynamic flowing.

It is imperative that you reserve any judgment calls about whether you want the job or not until after you leave the office. Separate your thoughts and cram any interview-related emotions or negativity you have towards the company, people, or job, into a box to separate it from the moment of the interview.

145

Don't try to process anything until you depart. Your one and only job is to do everything you can to convince the interviewers that this is the one and only company you want to work for, and this job gives you the opportunity to put your career assets to use as a company benefit. Pour it on so there's nothing left when you walk out. By holding back, you are hurting yourself and not giving the interview a fair shot.

Proactive career managers see interviews as incredibly valuable learning experiences that teach us about ourselves, learn from our mistakes, improve our interviewing skills, and discover how we can position ourselves to prospective employers. This is the epic moment where we communicate our career assets as solutions to an employer's staffing problem.

BE IN THE KNOW: WHAT EMPLOYERS ARE NOT ALLOWED TO ASK

Right now, there are a lot of job seekers who have been out of work for awhile and are starting to get desperate.

But if this sounds like your situation, don't let your desperation or urgency overcome your good sense. Sometimes, employers cross a legal and moral line by asking a question that is inappropriate or illegal.

So what do you do?

On one hand, you desperately need the money and will practically do anything to get a job that pays the bills.

But conversely, if the interview is where everyone is supposed to be on their best behavior (employer included), and the employer is demonstrating bad judgment by asking illegal questions, then do you really want to work there? It could be an indicator of a toxic work environment.

Or is it?

For organizations that have an established human resources department with clear policies and procedures, a question that is out of line truly is a rarity. The professional in that position usually takes exceptional care to make sure all legal requirements are followed to mitigate company exposure to potential lawsuits.

But, for the smaller "mom and pop" operations, oftentimes, where there isn't a specific human resource department, that means that the owner or manager is the one going through the interview process, and oftentimes, it's more of a muddling affair than a neutral, professional approach.

That's where some of these managers get into trouble by asking the wrong question, albeit unintentionally (or even on purpose) which lead to violation of state and federal employment laws.

As a job seeker, you have to try and determine what the background of the hiring scenario is and make some calculated decisions if you find yourself in the awkward position of being asked an illegal question.

Should you answer it or not?

Being forewarned is also being forearmed, and going into an interview knowing specifically what constitutes a legal question is extremely empowering.

In general, any question that inquiries directly to a person's age, arrest record, citizenship, family status, marital status, military background, national origin, religion or creed, membership, residence, relatives, race or color, sex, name, photographs, pregnancy, disability, workers' compensation, or sexual orientation are illegal.

There are certain permissible inquiries for each, but many of them can only be asked either when a job offer is being extended and this is part of the application process, or asked around those issues.

For a specific list of illegal questions and appropriate ones that employers may ask, you should consult your state employment, wage and hour division, or human services departments for a detailed list. There are also many resources on the Internet that can be referenced as well.

However, if you find yourself at the end of a question that leaves you squirming at the illegality of it, you have three options.

- **Choose to answer the specific question.**

By ignoring the illegality of the question, you are putting yourself at risk with your answer as a candidate, as the employer may have a hidden agenda. Plus you are condoning their behavior by replying.

- **Choose not to answer it.**

Instead, be assertive and state: "I don't see how this question impacts my ability to do the job," or, "I should alert you that this question is actually illegal under federal and state employment laws." You can always refuse to answer the question, which is perfectly within your rights, but obviously, the employer will likely take this the wrong way, perceive you as confrontational, and not to hire you as a result.

- **Choose to answer the question by providing an answer that pertains specifically to the job.**

Examine the intent of the question and respond to that instead of the bumbled question itself. Example: The employer asks if you are a U.S. citizen (illegal question) but you respond: "I am authorized to work in the United States."

These responses require some quick thinking and assessment as to how badly you need the job versus how well are you doing in the interview up until this point. There is risk involved, all the way around. By being well-informed as to your rights, you'll have a better chance of deciding how to best handle the situation, should it come up.

IS THERE A CULTURE FIT?

Remember, you are interviewing the employer as much as they are interviewing you. If you are actively managing your career, making the wrong move could set you back both in terms of income and advancement, not to mention any mental anguish you might suffer in a toxic work environment.

Your job, as the interviewer of the interviewers, is to find out what kind of culture fit there might be and walk away from ones that spell trouble from the outset.

If representatives from the prospective employer exhibit inappropriate or illegal behavior in the interview (as mentioned in the previous section), you need to realize that this could be just the tip of the iceberg and could be an indicator of what the daily work environment is like.

Most employers care about creating a healthy workplace, and would avoid asking such questions during the interview, especially since there is a great deal of legal risk involved in asking illegal questions during that process.

Understanding your rights can help you be assertive in an interview, and protect yourself from bad employment decisions down the road.

Talk to any career or human resource professional, and you'll likely get a wide range of definitions.

However, one thing holds absolutely true no matter what:

Company culture can define a business.

Companies that have a positive work brand presence attract people who want to work for them.

You've seen those examples on the news: Google has playrooms and goof-off space. Nike has a large campus and gym with a giant track surrounding it.

Ooooo. Sweeeeeeeet!

Wouldn't it be great to work at those companies?

But let's take a little closer look at what company culture really means.

Companies that champion emotional intelligence in their leaders cultivate trust and loyalty within staff. The ones that succeed in building a superior company culture have built a strong reputation for respecting and recognizing employees, which in turn, attracts top talent.

Perks are nice, but individual recognition and connection of talent to task matter more, and leaders who are savvy enough to be in tune with their employees' needs can successfully guide development of the company culture into fun.

Another aspect of management creating a positive workplace is through reinforcement of the value of the tasks assigned to employees. Personnel take pride in their individual ownership of job responsibilities. In a perfect scenario, the most important person is the one who is at the front line; a good company culture will make the receptionist feel that they count and have a personal stake in the company's success (which they do, and so does everyone else).

But where does company culture really begin, at least where job seekers are concerned?

Plugging into a company's culture can be a tough task for an outsider (job seeker). Here are some tips to gain confidence on assessing this fit during the interview.

- **Build the major connecting bridge.**
Fitting within a company's workplace culture means finding a link between your background and demonstrating a common vision and passion for their organizational mission, and this process begins in the interview.

You need to connect your assets to their mission to make the first big plug-in to their culture; personal values linking to company ones are like a marriage... there has to be a solid match from the start (but there is always room for some compromise).

- **Read the lay of the land for potential landmines in a company's culture.**
On one hand, hiring managers are looking for chemistry, personality, and genuine ability to fit into an already-established culture paradigm that you must be able to fit into.

But on the other hand, cues about this culture are difficult for job seekers to pick up on because no one is going to out-and-out tell you the way things really are like on the inside.

Job seekers can find out a great deal in the interview by watching the interviewers carefully. Who defers to whom? Are there sideways glances? Does someone cut someone else off? Do they seem happy to be there? Are you greeted cheerfully when arriving for your appointment? Trust your intuition on the "vibe" if you rely on your gut instinct, most of the time you'll find that you are reading the situation correctly.

- **Transparency impacts company culture.**

Learn what you can from your inside contacts and also during the interview. Don't be afraid to ask how previous organizational challenges have been handled. How the executive level handles significant strategy shifts or restructuring initiatives is indicative of that company's core culture values and overall treatment of staff.

- **Communication styles matter.**

Communication is another broad term, but think about it: What clues do you pick up on during the pre- and post-interview contact with the employer? Are the interviewers clear? Do they make you feel comfortable and well-informed? Or is it more ambush-style? How do the interviewers respond during your face-to-face interview? Is it a stiff conversation, or more of an open, easy communication style? Companies with positive cultures have leaders who are open to new ideas and are focused on empowering their employees. Communication styles that allow for free expression of thoughts, ideas, and suggestions in a constructive way without negative repercussions are good indicators of what a company culture is like.

- **What interviewers like about their jobs speaks volumes about corporate culture.**

Ho hum. If the interviewers are not fired up about what they do, how on earth do they expect to draw top talent? No one wants to work at a place when the interviewers can't even sell them on the benefits of working there.

One of the advantages to consider includes an upbeat work environment. People who are passionate about their jobs positively bubble enthusiasm and are excited to answer this important job seeker question. Staff will provide insights on important cultural benefits of working at this company. If they are happy, they'll be providing a cultural transmission of happiness throughout the interview, and you'll pick up on this right away.

- **If it doesn't fit, don't try to wear it.**

Ever make a mistake and take a job that you needed but once you got in there, you realized that you were not going to fit in? It could be the result of a complete culture clash, or realizing after the fact that the supervisor that you are reporting to is your worst nightmare. If you have picked up on any negative vibes during the interview, and can afford to walk away from that job, be fearless, and do it.

Ultimately, in the long run, you have to weigh the mental costs with the compensation… is it worth it? Some people rally and bravely try to make a go of it, but come to the understanding that this position is not meant to be.

Defining a company's culture is sometimes like trying to tackle a marshmallow… you can't quite get your arms around it and you aren't quite sure what you are going to get once you are inside. The best you can do is be smart, do your research, take a temperature "check" during the interview, and base your decision there. An accurate understanding of what are the key values of a company can help you plug in quickly and become welcomed as part of the team.

NEVER UNDERESTIMATE THE POWER OF A THANK YOU NOTE

One of the most important aspects of conducting a job search is remembering to thank everyone who has either interviewed or helped you.

But we all know the drill on what happens.

Someone helps us along the way, and in the back of our mind, we think, "Oooooh, I should send them a thank you note…" and then life happens. Kids need to get to soccer practice, you've got a new job lead you are following up on, and there's that meeting you need to get to... the result is that time slips by quickly.

...And then you realize a week or so later, "Gee, I really should have sent that thank you..."

And you are absolutely right. You should have.

But you didn't.

More importantly, what you have lost is much more than an opportunity to thank someone. You've also lost an opportunity to demonstrate your integrity as a person.

Taking a moment to express appreciation isn't necessarily expected nor required, but it does set people apart and say a lot about you. Those who take a moment to jot down a quick note (or email) and send via snail mail shows that you care, have attention to detail, and are eager to build a relationship with a person... and not just scramble over the top of them on your climb up the career ladder.

By not thanking someone, the person who went to bat for you only hears silence. And when you fail to thank those who are going to great lengths to help you succeed, the likelihood of them helping you out again plummets to practically zero.

Most people who get "burned" don't take the time to try and educate the person that asked for their help on what it was that they did wrong. And that's when you never hear from them again or find out why they don't really try to help you again.

NOTHING SAYS "HIRE ME" LIKE "THANK YOU"
THANK-YOU NOTE ETIQUETTE

22%
of employers are less likely to hire a candidate if they don't send a thank-you note after the interview.

86%
said it shows a lack a follow-through.

56%
said it indicates that the candidate isn't really serious about the position.

89%
said it is ok to send a thank-you note in the form of an email.

careerbuilder·

Source: 2011 CareerBuilder Survey of Hiring Managers

Image courtesy of CareerBuilder.com

It doesn't take much to find a moment and acknowledge the favor or the person. A simple, "Wow, thank you so much for (insert whatever the person did for you here)" always will suffice. This does not need to be a long essay.

Pushed on time? Buy a blank packet of "thank you notes" the next time when you are at the store. When checking out, buy some stamps. It's that easy.

Simple, quick, and effective.

You need to build your fan base of professional colleagues... because you never know when everything will circle back and you might need their help again.

People have long memories of those who took what they needed from you and never took the time to say thank you... it's a powerful tool in any job search.

Job Interview Autopsies: What You Don't Know Will Hurt You

We've all had that awful job interview where either we bobbled a question someone tossed at us (such as: "If you could be any animal, what would you be?") or we gave a bad answer and afterwards, we smack our foreheads because we realized we could have given a much better answer.

I talk to a lot of people who are stressed out about interviews and loathe them because they've had bad ones... many say they would rather have a root canal than go through the painful examination of an interview.

But you know what?

Interviews are actually good for you.

Why?

Think about it. They put us on the spot in a way that we usually don't encounter on a daily basis. An interview is actually a very powerful experience because you learn how you react under pressure.

If you really want to get over those jitters, you'll need to do an autopsy to discover what you need to know and/or work on to improve your skills in these situations.

Here are some tips on becoming more comfortable.

- **Interview often.**
Practice makes perfect. The more you do it, the more it's like staying on your bike. And if you do happen to fall, it'll be a lot easier to get back on again.

- **Write down all the questions you can remember after the interview.**
By keeping a running list of real interview questions you've encountered, you gain skill in knowing what might be coming your way the next time you interview with an employer.

- **Do your research.**
Did the employer field a question to you that had something to do with the company? If you had done your research, confidence comes with knowledge and even buys you some time. Sometimes, even deflecting those questions with similar but different detailed information can help you wiggle out of tight spots.

- **What was your gut instinct about the interview?**
Trusting your intuition is important… if you are feeling not-so-great about an interview and your performance in there, there might have

been something non-verbal that the interviewers were exuding that put you off. If you aren't walking out pumped up and energized, is this really the right opportunity for you?

If you don't take the time to truly examine how you performed in an interview, and don't dissect the pieces that you did well versus the ones in which you had an #epicfail, you won't learn about yourself nor will you learn what you can do better next time. In your lifetime, you'll have a lot more interviews than job offers, so mastering the knowledge of your strengths and weak points is incredibly important to your career... otherwise, what you don't know will hurt you.

What Happens When You Do Everything Right In An Interview... And The Hiring Manager Is Nuts?

Have you ever had this happen to you?

REAL-WORLD EXAMPLE
"Emily," a client and a friend of mine, recently had a rattling experience. She applied for a job for which she was eminently qualified, and executed everything flawlessly throughout the entire job application and interview process... including doing her research on the company, preparing interview questions of her own, writing thank you notes, and then politely checking in on the status of her application to show just the right level of interest and enthusiasm for the position.

But when she made it to the second round (after having charmed the first-round interview panel), she found herself sitting in front of a company vice president who was the final decision-maker...and someone who also was clearly off of her rocker.

From inappropriate personal items on display in the VP's office to mention of being under the influence of a painkiller, to a rambling tirade that lasted 45 minutes of the 55-minute long interview, Emily found it difficult to get a word in edgewise to connect her background to the position opening. The conversation with the VP bounced all over the place, and it was clear that the VP had some serious personal mental issues.

The whole "interview" ended up being a monologue from the VP, and at that point, Emily realized that it was best to resign herself to letting the VP take the conversation where she wanted to take it... which was apparently all over the map.

This whole situation was incredibly discouraging for Emily. She was fired up, had great ideas to take the organization to the next level, had gotten the buy-in from the other staff in the first-round, and was ready to hit the ground running. Everything was electrified with the "YES, I can do it" vibe.

Yet it was clear that there was one problem that the department was not able to deal with...

The VP was nuts.

And sure enough, in a follow up call to HR a week later, Emily was told that the VP had said that she was going to get back to Emily personally (but did not).... and the HR person sympathetically told Emily that the VP had selected two other candidates for a third round, and suddenly, had gone in an entirely different direction in terms of candidate requirements (at this point, the HR person had a tinge of irritation in her voice).

Crushed, Emily hung up, trying to figure out what to make of the entire experience.

So what do you do, when everything is game, set, and match: and then the loose cannon arrives on the scene and blows everything to bits… and there is nothing you or anyone else who is your advocate can do?

- **You cannot control the situation.**
As frustrating as it is, that person/obstacle is immovable and they are in a position of authority which you cannot change. You are only responsible for your conduct, and if you execute everything flawlessly, then you've done everything expected and demanded of you.

Beyond that, there is absolutely nothing else that you can do to influence or shift opinion, and to attempt to do so will only result in it reflecting badly on you for circumventing the person in question.

- **You need to let it go.**

Look through the entire experience and determine the take-aways… is there anything you could have done better? It's okay to examine what happened, what the clues were, how you responded, and if there was anything else you could have contributed differently – but you ultimately cannot dwell on it… you'll drive yourself crazy with "what ifs."

Decide what you want to learn from the experience and integrate it into how you want to present yourself, should this same situation present itself again. Then let it go, and concentrate your efforts on your job search efforts. Don't devote your energy to something that is now in the past… instead, focus on the future.

- **You wouldn't have enjoyed working there anyway.**
Sure, it's easy to adopt this attitude, but think of it this way… how many of us end up in a dysfunctional workplace that eats up our productivity time by "kivetching" to other employees about a particular problem or person?

If you are experiencing a disconnect in the interview and can easily see through personal issues and personality problems of your potential future boss, what do you think it would be like on a daily basis?

Most likely, it won't improve from there... Remember that you are interviewing employers just as much as they are interviewing you. If the employer is that bad in an interview, what do you think they will be like as your boss?

And, as part of evaluating a job opportunity, no matter how much you need the money, you should weigh the mental cost of working with supervisors with control, anger, or personal issues. A healthy workplace could be more desirable than a bigger paycheck served up with a whole lot of angst. And chances are that there's someone in your social or work circle that ended up going to counseling because of an unhealthy work environment.

The key to getting beyond these excruciatingly disappointing interviews where you knew you had it "in the bag" but got derailed by someone who isn't in their right mind is to understand the boundary between what you can and cannot control, and to do what you can do to the best of your ability.

If it doesn't come to fruition, then there wasn't a fit, and you need to move on to the next opportunity and put your energy into more pro-ductive efforts.

HOW YOU INTERVIEW GOES BEYOND THE CURRENT OPENING

The ultimate outcome of an interview isn't necessarily whether you got the job or not. Too much emphasis is put on this usually because we are so focused on the short-term. What happens is that we leave an inter-view feeling as though it is the only thing that matters, but in reality, the interview can impact your career destiny in different ways.

How we conduct ourselves during the entire process can affect our personal brand and either validate or negate what people's existing perceptions of us. Active career managers realize that the job might not have been the right opportunity, but the long-term view is that how you conduct yourself throughout the entire process will have far-reaching impacts on your future career prospects.

- **You may be contacted for future openings.**

Candidates that impress on the first go-around are definitely kept on file for future reference, should another opening be posted.

- **You may get referred to others.**

Employers talk to their counterparts, and while their job opening may now be closed, if you did a good job and are on top of their mind as an excellent second choice, you might be pleasantly surprised to find out that they will refer you to colleagues who are in a similar talent search.

It goes something like this: Company A: "Yeah, well, we are looking for a new IT manager and haven't even started the process yet." Company B: "Really? We just hired one here and I have to tell you, it was a tough choice. We had two great candidates and could only hire one." Company A: "Really? Would you mind passing on that person over to me? I'd like to talk to them."

- **How you handle rejection matters.**

You will interview for countless more jobs than you will ever actually be hired for, so rejection will happen. How you handle it will be a deciding factor for future potential jobs.

The people you interact with remember you better if you exhibit grace, empathy, and class, versus dejection and anger. If you can stay positive despite the current job opening not working out, and show that you are still genuinely interested in the company, you are leaving very positive feelings behind with those decision makers.

- **If the first candidate doesn't work out, you want to be an easy second choice.**

As much probing and checking an employer might do, sometimes their first choice doesn't work out. Perhaps that person has accepted employment elsewhere or declined for some reason... or maybe they did take the job and it simply didn't work out. Because of this, sometimes employers will delve right back into the applications from the first round. If you play your cards right, you want to come immediately to mind if candidate No. 1 doesn't pan out.

- **Send a thank you note... even after being declined an offer.**

The staffing firm Accountemps conducted a survey of executives in 2007 that found that 49% of all job seekers fail to send a thank you note. Most people that follow this formality send it immediately after an interview.

But what about sending a thank you note after getting rejected? The odds plummet at that point. But taking the time to reaffirm your interest in the company and ask to be considered for future positions might be a great way to take what most people see as a negative and spin it into a positive.

- **Stay in touch.**

At tastefully planned intervals, you can appropriately follow up with interviewers with whom you built rapport to keep your brand in circulation with them.

For example, if you see an article a month or so after the interview that might be of interest to them, forward it to them. Include a short note saying, "Just saw this and it reminded me about _____ that we talked about when I came in for an interview. Enjoy!"

Overcome any negative feelings you might have by not being offered the job and do everything you can to make the employer's interaction and impression of you a good one. It could make the difference for any future applications you make with that company.

TIME TO PLAY POKER

PLAYING TO WIN: HOW NEGOTIATIONS CAN AFFECT YOUR CAREER LEVEL AND PAY FOR YEARS TO COME

"There are no secrets to success. It is the result of preparation, hard work, and learning from failure."
- Colin Powell

There are only a few things that we do on occasion that can have deep impacts on every facet of our lives. All involve negotiation. Are you buying a car? Are you buying a house? Are you wooing a potential partner or spouse?

Chances are you've spent more time preparing for those big moments than you have getting ready to duke it out on the salary negotiation mat with a prospective employer.

Coming to an agreement on salary is nerve-wracking, yet so much is at stake. Why is that we spend more time investigating and preparing for the other decisions in our life, and hardly any time on how we are going to negotiate our way into a salary level that will provide better financial security. This can also have a big effect on our job satisfaction as we have strong feelings about getting compensated for the value of our work.

The reason why salary negotiation is so tough is because we are finally putting a dollar amount on what we are actually worth.

This monetary justification makes the negotiation even more personal and difficult, but should be something you should be proud of and embrace, instead of shying away from it.

We want and *should* command the highest, most competitive salary that we can which is equal to that of our peers, and competitive for our specific job area.

However, the nation's economy can wreak havoc on even the best-planned salary negotiations… depending on if it is a sellers' or buyers' market.

When the economy is doing well and companies are flush with cash, they might be more willing to shell out higher salary levels to attract and retain the right talent as part of a bidding war where the job seeker has the advantage.

The flip side of that scenario is when the economy tanks, jobs are scarce, and cash is tight. Then the employer is in the catbird seat and has more leverage in negotiating the final amount downward due to job seeker desperation to find any job.

From a business standpoint, employers look at salary negotiation as trying to hire the best-level talent for the lowest price... their job is to keep overhead costs down, not pay you extra money out of the goodness of their heart. Don't ever lose sight of the fact that your presence at a company is purely a business decision; nothing more, and nothing less. Your task, however, is to negotiate your worth as it factors into that business decision.

Employers have set compensation budgets and in a tight job market, they possess even less patience for candidates who decide to play games in an effort to win higher pay.

The end result is two diametrically-opposed sides and an expectation to meet somewhere in the middle. And in truth, that's usually where the final result lands.

Consider this: How you negotiate your salary and compensation can impact you for years to come when you think about the cumulative earnings you realize.

Negotiate badly, and you could set yourself back substantially behind your peers, not to mention feeling crummy about the whole deal. Never underestimate how this can nibble away at your psyche and affect how you perceive your job and overall performance levels. If you aren't happy and feel that you are excessively underpaid, you'll be less motivated because you don't feel as though the company values what you contribute.

Negotiate smartly, and you concentrate your efforts on being as productive as possible and likely have a much higher level of job satisfaction. And you are in a better position, salary-wise, to negotiate even higher compensation when you make your next job move.

KNOW YOUR VALUE

Many companies refuse to publish a salary range for a job posting, mainly in an attempt to "fish" around to see what they might catch and for what price. That leaves you somewhat in the dark as to what their bottom line is and whether you should even bother throwing your hat in the ring or not.

It's a delicate dance in which candidates are trying to figure out what the employer wants to pay while company decision makers are trying to figure out how much they can hire the candidate for.

And no one wants to show their cards.

If there is not any stated salary information published with the job posting, you have to take things into your own hands. There are some salary calculator tools you can use to get a general ballpark of what the employer might (or should be) paying to be at a competitive wage.

Many state and national trade associations have white papers or reports on competitive salaries for positions within that field.

Websites like Glassdoor.com, Payscale.com, indeed.com/salary, CBsalary. com, or Salary.com can provide an approximation of what salaries are, with regional adjustments.

Additionally, based on what you have been paid in the past combined with any other similar job announcements where the salary levels are revealed, you should start to have a pretty good general idea of what the company is paying for that specific position.

The next step means that you need to figure out where you fall inside the range. Of course, we all want to be at the top level, but most of us don't make it by a long shot. You have to have a solid understanding of your abilities and what you think an honest acceptable range would be.

These numbers need to include what the lowest acceptable number might be as well as the highest amount you can reasonably expect to receive if you negotiate hard.

The other thing you need to factor in that most people don't think about is the overall compensation package. Job seekers tend to zero in on the salary, but when benefits and retirement funds are included, the number actually gets bigger. With more and more employees paying more for their health care, looking at the big picture and what might be negotiable changes that overall compensation amount as well.

Think about the whole package and what you hope to gain... what is a priority? It might mean a lower salary level but you can claim your dependents on the health insurance. Or more vacation time.

Ultimately, you have to decide what is right and best for your particular situation, before you even walk into a negotiation process.

KNOW WHEN TO TALK SALARY

It is important to know that a classic mistake by job seekers is to initiate the salary discussion before it is appropriate. The general rule of thumb about salary discussions is to only get into this area when a bonafide job offer is being made. Having a salary conversation before this point is premature, and can convey the wrong message about you.

Sometimes, as part of the "fishing" game, job seekers are asked to provide their salary history or requirements as part of the application process before they are even selected for an interview.

The purpose of this tactic can be two-fold: To weed out people outside of the company's ballpark or to remove any negotiation power later, should you be selected to be interviewed and later offered the job.

Unfortunately, this has become the bane of job applicant experiences applying online, where this information is literally forced out.

There are two options for handling this situation... you can either put in the absolute lowest number you would be willing to accept (which will hopefully be within the employer's range and not rule you out as being too high) – OR – you can put down a reasonable number somewhere in the middle of your range that you figured out previously.

Written applications are a little easier. Under the box where you are asked what your final salary was at the previous company, you could choose to leave this area blank, which may result in an employer tossing your application out completely. Another option is to put in "To be discussed later," or you can fill in a range, which runs the same risk.

However, if getting your salary history is so important to the employer that they would take a highly qualified candidate out of the running, this should be a warning sign that they are more concerned about budget than quality... and is a good reason for you to keep looking.

It should also be noted that you should *never* bring up any of your personal financial constraints or pressures during the salary discussion itself. The employer is under no obligation to help you, and your personal financial situation does not concern them.

In fact, by revealing personal fiscal issues, you could be causing concern about your ability to handle money, which could spill over to the work environment... if you can't manage your personal budget, then why would the company be willing to let you be in charge of a project or departmental one?

The Poker Game Begins... With Your Financial Future

So what happens if an employer directly asks you in the interview to tell them how much money you made in your previous jobs?

Many unemployed people are so desperate that they cave in right away for fear that they might not get the job if they don't "play nice" in the employer's cat-and-mouse game of salary negotiation.

Have you experienced this at some point in your career? Then you know the drill. You are in the hot seat for an interview, things are getting towards a definite "close" and it is clear that a deal is now in the works.

Then the employer drops their bomb in an interview by casually asking, "So, what are your salary needs?" or "What are you earning currently?"

So, it all comes down to this moment. Time to deal the cards and start playing strategically... what you do now completely impacts your financial earnings over the course of your entire career.

So what is a job applicant to do? What are your options?

Here are several approaches you can take when it comes down to handling the thorny issue of salary negotiation in an interview. There isn't any "perfect" way to negotiate because each situation is subjective to the company culture and the person interviewing you/making the hiring decision.

Being educated about your options and also having a good "read" on the internal company environment can help provide you with the necessary business intelligence on the best way to approach this discussion.

- **Give them what they want.**

Know when the chips are down and the employer is fixated on a specific answer to the salary question. If the job opportunity truly hinges on whether you give them an answer to this question, then you have to make the decision whether to divulge your salary to give them what they want or not.

The obvious downside to providing that specific number is that now you have absolutely no negotiating room whatsoever. The company knows exactly what they can "get" you for, salary-wise, and it will be very difficult to go upwards at this point.

- **Provide a range.**

Do your research on what is a reasonable expectation for salary for the type of position for which you are applying. Then make your move by providing a similar range, with your current salary level somewhere inside that bracket. Depending on what you are willing to accept (even if it is below your most recent earning level), make sure the upper number isn't in outer orbit... otherwise you can quickly get tossed out due to a too-high salary requirement.

- **Dodge #1: Let's talk later.**

Until a job offer is actually on the table, any preliminary discussion of salary is actually a ploy. The employer is testing the waters to see if there is a match between their salary number and yours. Proactively stepping into the discussion can work for you if you know this tactic will work. A good way of framing it nicely: "Until a job offer is being made, I would like to request that this discussion take place later... right now, I am very interested in learning more about this job and how I can help your company."

- **Dodge #2: We're in the same ballpark.**

Again, you can be assertive while dishing out a compliment that holds them accountable: "I am confident that your company offers an industry-competitive wage and with that understanding, I know we'll be able to reach a compromise once we get into actual negotiations."

- **Dodge #3: My last job didn't reflect all the duties I would be doing in this position.**

Use this approach to counter an employer's attempt to extrapolate what you earned previously into what they want to pay for this position. Say something along the lines of, "We should look at the difference between the two positions in order to assess the additional responsibilities beyond my last job, and come up with a fair level of compensation." Using these words places the burden on the prospective employer to work within the confines of what must be fair… anything else will make them look unreasonable.

- **Dodge #4: Redirect.**

If they insist on knowing your salary before making an offer and won't budge, then redirect the question back to them… "I am really excited about this position and would appreciate it if you could make me an offer based on what you have already budgeted for this position. Based on that amount, I am confident we can find some mutually agreeable terms."

- **Force their hand… instead of yours.**

Acknowledge that they have a set budget (whatever that may be) for this position, and then ask them, based on how the interview has gone for them, what they think your value would be to the company. This is very powerful because you are testing their interest in you as well as forcing them to quantify what they think you are worth.

- **Don't let them sabotage you.**

With so many people out of work these days, chances are that there are candidates who would be considered "overqualified." If you fall under that description, the employer may be searching for a way to rule you out based on an assumption that higher qualifications mean that you will expect higher pay. That might not be the case for you, so don't let them take you down that road. Instead, acknowledge that while salary is important, it is only one facet about the job that is important to you. Take the opportunity to talk about the parts of the job that get you fired up to redirect attention away from the "overqualified" statement and away from the higher pay hang-up.

- **Avoid the issue.**

This is a tactic some people take because A) They don't really know how to handle it or B) They assume that by avoiding it, the employer won't notice that the candidate didn't address the question. All of which can completely and utterly backfire. Salary numbers are absolutely going to be a hot button for an employer, and they'll be specifically scanning for that reference mentioning your salary history in the cover letter.

- **Remember: They are interested in you... which equals leverage.**

The fact that you've been called into an interview and are starting to talk salary means that things are looking good from their end.

The culmination of your impressive résumé, superior interviewing skills, chemistry, and answers that resonate with them are actually stoking their fires, so keeping in mind that you are a commodity that they are now desiring does give you leverage in the negotiation process. If they negotiate badly, the employer's fear is that you could potentially be snapped up by a competitor. Don't be afraid to stand pat and hold your ground.

These salary discussion techniques are all options you can exercise based on your personal read and feel for how the interview is going. But there is one constant you should be aware of: *Never* lie about your salary... this is something that is easily verifiable and if you make an attempt to over-inflate what your actual earnings have been, you could be exposed as a liar and for misrepresenting yourself for financial gain. Not exactly a compelling reason to complete the hiring process.

CREDIT: Special reprint permission from John McPherson from
"Close to Home" for use in this book

The most successful tricks to negotiating your salary is being flexible, willing to negotiate on other options including benefits, having a good knowledge of what jobs of this type typically pay, and being centered on what your value is without being overconfident.

In the long run, if you take a positive, collaborative approach in negotiating your salary, chances are that the employer will respond positively, and you'll be happier because you kept your cards close to your chest while keeping up your poker face. It could mean a substantial long-term gain in overall career earnings if you are smart and savvy about how you negotiate your next salary.

BENEFITS AND VACATION TIME

Most people don't factor in benefits to their overall compensation package. They automatically get hung up on salary and forget that non-cash benefits such as health insurance, vacation time, extra time away (paid/ unpaid), mileage, employer matches to 401k programs, gym memberships, and use of company vehicle or car allowance (if available), to name a few, are just as important.

With health costs skyrocketing and employees being asked to cover more of their insurance, this could be another area you could look at negotiating. Every employee should be aware of how much it costs to have health insurance, so you can know whether the benefits offered in the negotiation are acceptable or not. If you overlook this area, you could potentially end up shelling out more money out of pocket than in previous jobs, and actually cut your overall net earnings.

The same goes for vacation time. Sometimes employers are unwilling to budge on the salary level for the position, but there might be an opportunity for you to counteroffer with a request for another week of vacation time instead, which means no additional out-of-pocket expense to the employer beyond the budgeted compensation level.

But what happens when you have a vacation that you've paid for (including airline tickets and other expenses), and right before you are packing your bags, a miracle happens and a job offer comes along?

Tough call. Ironically, many people say that in order to land a job offer, all you have to do is schedule a vacation. Then presto! The phone starts ringing.

Whether this is really true or not, you shouldn't mention vacation plans during the interview phase until it is clear that a job offer is in the works. Once that happens, there comes a point where you need to make some decisions.

The question on how to handle this situation comes up frequently, and there are a couple of ways to deal with it, especially since you have already sunk in a pretty good chunk of change investing in much-needed R&R.

- **Drop everything and cancel your plans.**
That sounds rather dramatic, but then again, if you have been looking for work for an extended period of time, it would be a relief to have a job…so those vacation plans, no matter how tempting, can wait. If you opt to cancel those plans, however, don't mention it to the employer. They should not be made to feel that they have caused you an inconvenience. If you cancel your vacation, keep mum about any cancelled plans and instead focus on getting acclimated with the new job and savoring the moment of being the top candidate.

- **Start looking into options to shift vacation dates around.**
Sometimes, you have flexibility and can either rebook later or get a credit. It might be worth saving the vacation time for later once your

new work schedule gets smoothed out and you have the actual time to take off. Don't mention this situation to the employer because it really doesn't concern them!

- **If your plans are non-cancellable or exceptionally complex (as in involving other people), be up front.**

Employers hate surprises. Before you sign on to the company, you should absolutely mention that you have another commitment coming up. Most companies are aware that they aren't the center of the universe and there is a high likelihood that the new employee probably has some pre-existing commitments that may affect their initial schedule after joining the company. Be up front, mention the dates and general nature of the request, and ask how the employer prefers to work around this. Most will be willing to work with you and be flexible.

- **Least preferable: "The Last Stand."**

It may come down to this: After disclosing your conflict, the employer says: Cancel the plans. The obstacle: You don't want to or can't. Time for a stand-off, which isn't the best way to start off on the right foot with an employer, to say the least. The company holds the upper hand, with the job carrot dangling in front of you, but this offer can evaporate if they sense trouble or difficulty in accepting it on your end.

I've never actually heard of anyone ditching a job offer in favor of a vacation, but stranger things have happened. You may find resistance from the employer after disclosing pre-existing plans, and it is possible that you end up in the position of not being very happy and taking a loss on the vacation. That means you aren't very pleased, either, and can provide an insight into the company management culture that you might not like.

Other Things To Consider...

If an employer truly is focused on hiring you and the salary range isn't within your requirements, sometimes they will offer a signing bonus which is a one-time payment which acknowledges that you are worth more than what the position is paying as a statement of goodwill from the employer. If the negotiations are getting stuck with no agreement in sight, you could ask: "What is the signing bonus if I decide to come on board?" which indicates you are willing to compromise if they are.

Another thing to consider is if you are going to be traveling a lot with your job, how will expense reimbursements be handled? Will you have a corporate credit card issued in your name or be paid out of pocket then submit expense reports? Many companies go the expense report route to reduce potential risk of employees abusing corporate credit cards. You should get clarity on how this will be handled, and within what timeframe.

As someone who had a lot of business travel to Europe for a previous employer, I frequently had $1,000-$5,000 monthly credit card bills. But unfortunately, the accounting department didn't process my expense reports for 45+ days which forced me to play financial roulette with my personal savings account to pay off bills on time... while waiting for my reimbursement check to be finally cut.

This is an important thing to think about because, depending on how many expenses you might be incurring for work, it could play havoc with your own finances. So be aware about this possibility when negotiating a job offer.

Finally, probably the biggest area overlooked by candidates in the negotiation process is to secure some kind of commitment from the employer about their willingness to provide for your professional development. This is important to both parties because you are asking for the employer to make an investment into your ability to do a good job while at the same time enhancing your own professionalism and subject matter expertise.

People who are engaged in active career management are always thinking beyond just a salary during the negotiation process and are thinking about all the other areas of their employment which can also be negotiated as well. It could mean better quality of life and less stress as well!

COUNTER-OFFERS

Counter-offers from your current employer after you already have lined up another job are huge ego-boosters. Inside, you are thinking, "Wow, they really, really want me!" and it is very tempting to accept because it seems like a win-win situation. You get more pay or benefits, or perhaps more vacation time or even promises of promotions.

But someone who is on top of managing their career can see through the ego-flattering counter-offer and realize the negative impacts that accepting one would have on their career.

Good employers don't make counter-offers they know that you have already made your intentions clear by making the decision to leave the company. Smart career managers don't accept because by your current employer making a counter-offer, the company's hand is being forced, and that can result in bad feelings later on.

Consider the following factors during a counter-offer.

- **No one likes to be played for a fool.**
The new employer has spent a lot of time and energy during the recruitment and hiring process, and won't like being turned down. This doesn't

sit very well, no matter how competitive the counter-offer is from your current employer.

Some companies may interpret this as an attempt to use a bargaining chip to get what you want out of your current employer, with no real intention of ever leaving the company in the first place. Hiring managers have long memories, and keep track of these things. Don't play that game!

- **You've already broken employer trust.**

The fact that you have quietly been seeking employment elsewhere can also alert your current employer that you haven't been happy. This can raise questions about where your loyalties lie, and you should never have an employer ever question that. Additionally, you could be seen as a potential security risk as you have already made an employment foray outside of the company.

This may lead them to wonder about what you'll do the next time things aren't going your way… it also leaves a bad taste in their mouth by feeling that you forced their hand to cough up more money or benefits, and may put more pressure on you to perform in order to justify their move to keep you onboard.

- **Your departure could spur quick reactions that result in knee-jerk company decisions.**

The fear of losing you could induce the employer to make spur-of-the-moment decisions as to what they promise you. Do they plan to offer you a promotion? If so, are you really ready to step into that role?

The last thing you want to do is be offered a position of higher responsibility only to fail due to your lack of readiness to step into that role.

- **A counter-offer doesn't change why you wanted to leave in the first place.**

Usually, counter-offers are all about additional money or benefits, but not usually the root motivating factor as to why you started to look for work elsewhere. A counter-offer usually doesn't improve your working situation and can actually complicate it after being accepted. Co-workers are aware of the stunt you pulled and treat you like an outsider. Consider all the other factors that made you unhappy initially... is it the commute, hours, problem co-workers/boss, lack of career advancement, or lack of excitement? Or no new challenges? Think through these aspects carefully, and ask yourself if anything would change if you got paid more. The answer is likely "no."

- **By accepting, you have likely signed your own job death warrant.**

Now that the cat is out of the bag, your employer is negotiating in their own short-term interest. They need to buy time to keep you in the job to finish projects... while at the same time, they initiate their own search to replace you as soon as possible. It may seem like they are moving to keep you, but now they see you as expendable and are working quickly behind the scenes to squeeze what they need out of you until they line up someone to step into your job.

- **Everything could backfire and you end up with zip.**

It is entirely possible that your attempt in playing your current employer off the new one could cause the entire house of cards to fall... the new offer could be withdrawn and your boss could decide not to match it. Now, all of a sudden, what seemed like a very juicy situation has gone sour. You are out of a job and you have not one, but two, companies not seeing you in a favorable light.

Counter-offers are usually best dealt with by saying, "I appreciate and am extremely flattered by your generous offer, but I don't want to create the impression that I am trying to force you into retaining me as an employee. This is a new opportunity that I cannot refuse and know that you will understand and respect my decision."

What is born out of this comment is INTEGRITY. It may cause short-term hard feelings tied to your departure, but this actually takes a huge amount off the employer's shoulders so they don't have to scramble to make a lot of important decisions on very short notice.

THE CHIPS ARE DOWN... PLAYING YOUR CARDS RIGHT WHEN YOU ARE HOPING FOR/EXPECTING MORE THAN ONE JOB OFFER

We all know that timing is everything and that includes getting the right job offers at the right time.

Unfortunately, things don't always pan out like we hope, and it may come to pass that you receive a job offer from one company while holding out hope that the upcoming interview you have with your dream job at a different organization will put you in a better career direction.

So how do you handle this often difficult situation... to make you come out on top as a winner?

It's a tough question but what it really boils down to is that you need to buy yourself time. There is no guarantee that the dream job is even going to be offered to you... the interview has yet to even happen.

Proactively managing your career means that you absolutely need to have a clear idea of what each job could mean to your career. Take time to evaluate the pros and cons of what each position could mean to your career goals, and prioritize them accordingly. Depending on your financial needs or objectives, you may need to make some tough decisions if the timing of multiple offers doesn't line up in your favor.

TRANSFORM TEMP/CONTRACT WORK INTO A PERMANENT JOB

Great news! You've landed either temporary or contract work, which suddenly has taken so much stress off of you from looking for a job.

Now you can pay the bills, settle in, and concentrate your focus on getting up to speed and making valuable contributions.

But what's the worst thing that can happen at this point? Becoming complacent in this moment of opportunity.

But first, let's be clear. Contract or temporary work does *not* guarantee a future at the company. It is a stretch of employment that has a finite end to it, and you're going to have to deal with it sooner or later.

But despite not being a permanent employee, you have something vastly more powerful in your career arsenal right now than other job seekers.

You have a foot in the door.

You are a known quantity.

And you have a chance to prove yourself.

If you are seeking permanent work and accept part-time, contract, or temp employment, you should be focused on doing quality work as job No. 1, and looking for opportunities to secure a longer-term position within the employer as job No. 2.

There are several ways to position yourself and take advantage of this opportunity to potentially extend your employment with this company. Here are five tips on how to transform temporary or contract work into the possibility of you being retained as a full-time, regular employee.

- **Think and act like an employee genuinely interested in mission and bottom line of the company.**

If you just show up, do your job, and complete only the minimum of what is asked of you… well, you've just painted yourself into a very small box that doesn't show what you are capable of achieving. While you do have to be aware of not stepping on toes, if you truly find a new way to save the company money or help them in any way, make sure you let the key supervisor know. They'll appreciate it.

- **Provide status reports to all key stakeholders in a timely, concise way.**

Sometimes, as a temp/contract employee, you won't be seen as a regular part of the staff team and may get left out of the normal information flow. By taking the initiative on communications, you also demonstrate your strong skills in this area and provide critical updates to projects. Also ask to be copied on reports as well so you are up to speed with what others are working on at the same time.

- **If possible (and you can manage the added work), request additional tasks.**

This will give you a broader knowledge of company operations, strengthen your bench skills, bring you into more contact with a larger number of decision makers and co-workers, and most importantly, validates your initiative.

- **Ask to be hired full-time.**

If a staff opening for which you are qualified comes up while you are employed on a temp/contract basis, don't be afraid to talk to the key decision maker for that position to let them know about your interest in the job. You don't want to be too aggressive, but at the same time, this isn't the moment to suddenly be a wallflower and hope that they "pick" you. If you don't tell them of your interest, they won't ever know.

- **Propose a job if the timing is right.**

Many employers have cut back staffing to bare minimum due to the economy, but as things ease up a bit, they might be more receptive to reinstating previously cut positions. If the timing seems right, and you can identify a clear need which you can fulfill as a full time worker, schedule a time to talk to the decision maker and make your proposal.

If none of these tactics work, and the part-time/contract work has a concrete end date, then you should concentrate on doing the best job possible for the employer during your final stretch of employment there.

Then, several weeks before the scheduled end-date, set up a time with your supervisor, discuss your interest in their company and field, and if they seem willing, ask them about who they would recommend talking to about possible full-time employment in that same industry.

It also can't hurt to request a letter of reference.

Finally, always remember to thank them for the opportunity to work at their company, and make them feel that if a position were to come open, you would prefer to work at their organization based on the positive experience you've had while you've been there.

Proactive career managers see temporary or contract work as inroads to potential full-time work, and are able to see how they can positively leverage their experience, skills, and connections gained through that employment contract into their next opportunity.

7

YOU'RE HIRED...

WHY MANAGING YOUR CAREER DOESN'T END WITH A NEW JOB

"Accomplishing the impossible means only that the boss will add it to your regular duties."
- Doug Larson

Of course, any employer in their right mind would never add "accomplishing the impossible" to a job description for an opening at their company, but those expectations still remain.

The truth is that while you are excited about the new job, you really don't know what lies beyond the first day in terms of where you will go and what you will really be doing. The full scope of your work won't truly be revealed until you've actually gotten some experience at the new company under your belt.

Now that you have agreed to join a new company, transitioning between ending employment at one company and starting it at another can be tough.

This is when you need to pay close very close attention to every move you make to avoid any missteps that could interfere with your career management. And more importantly, you never know when the company where you used to work may return to you as a customer (or you might want to return to work for them), so don't ever burn bridges!

Giving Notice: Planning Your Exit Strategy

In the limbo between leaving one company and on-boarding to another, it's common to go through a wide array of mixed emotions. We may have really liked the people and environment so we are sad to go, while at the same time, there is a great deal of excitement and anticipation for the new challenge that lies ahead.

How you depart an employer actually says a lot about you… always aim to walk the high road and be gracious. It might be a horrible employment situation but if you were able to depart with class and integrity, it says a lot more about you than the company. And that's what matters!

The following are some important things to consider when giving notice which can help ease the process for both you and the employer you are leaving.

▪ **Talking to the boss.**
"The" moment will finally arrive where you knock on your supervisor's door and ask for a few minutes to talk. This is never an easy

190

conversation for either party and is often nerve-wracking, especially for the employee. Proceed with gentleness, measured confidence, and empathy for the employer's situation but do not get so caught up in guilt for leaving that you end up reconsidering your decision. Be positive and step carefully.

- **Sufficient notice.**

Providing sufficient notice to employers helps them maneuver around upcoming deadlines and mission-critical details, while minimizing disruptions to operations. Most employers appreciate having advance notice of employee departures, and will work around you during the transition time.

However, before you go into your boss' office, you should make sure you have all of your items consolidated as some companies now are immediately asking employees who give notice to leave the premises within minutes. Scrambling around and trying to gather things can be very disjointing, especially with security standing outside your cube, tapping their foot, waiting to escort you out the door.

Get your ducks in a row by quietly and unobtrusively segregating your personal effects from those belonging to the company... just in case. Hopefully, as a proactive career manager, you have already been maintaining records relating to your performance-to-goals, but in case you haven't, take time before you give your notice to dig up the information before you leave – once you do depart, it'll be infinitely more difficult to get specific metrics when you no longer have access to that data.

- **Discuss references and letter(s) of recommendation.**

You should be up front during your meeting with the boss. Be assertive by saying, "Based on my performance at this company, what kind of reference can I expect about the work I have done here?"You should ask this question during the discussion in order to find out how your time at the company will be discussed in the future. Hopefully, you will already know the answer before this point!

- **Bridge the job transition gap by offering consulting or part-time assistance.**

Depending on your circumstances, you might be able to negotiate a transition period where you work part-time or provide consulting services to the current employer while starting work at the new company. Usually, this is at the request of your current business, versus something you offer. But if they are in a jam and you are truly the only one who can pull all the ends together, this might be an option to win bonus points and go out on a very high note as the "hero" who stuck around to help out.

- **Suitable replacements.**

The first thought that goes through the supervisor's mind once you give notice is: "How I am going to fill this position?" Give some consideration to this problem posed to the employer by thinking ahead and identifying potential individuals who might be a good match both personality-wise and expertise-wise to the position that you are vacating.

Be ready to counter with the employer's initial shock to your resignation with, "Again, I have had an incredible experience working at this company but I realize that with my departure, you'll be short-handed. I've been doing some thinking, and perhaps (names of people) would be excellent replacements." Bingo. You have already cut the employer's anxiety down a notch. Sure, they will still want to go through their own recruitment process, but if you have already narrowed down the search for them, they know they have a back-up short list to rely upon.

- **Exit interviews (time to come clean?).**

Only you can get a "read" on company culture to know whether exit interviews are the appropriate place to provide feedback on your experience working at the organization.

Do them poorly and vent in what you think is a safe environment, and it could backfire on you by burning bridges.

Do them right, and an employer genuinely interested in improving the workplace will gladly take your objective feedback into consideration.

A lot of how successful exit interviews end up has to do with the relationship that you have with the supervisor. Are they someone you trust? Do you feel comfortable providing feedback? You'll need to proceed with caution when entering this territory.

No matter how you address the situation, you should make sure to include more platitudes than complaints. Remember to compliment the company and talk about the many things you learned and benefited from in addition to the top wins that you achieved while there. Then drop a short comment, "One thing that I think could be improved upon is _____, which can be achieved by _____." Adopting the problem-solution approach is smart because you are offering insight to an issue while offering a way to fix it.

- **Notice to internal and external stakeholders.**
During the time when you give your notice, you should discuss with your supervisor how people should be notified about your departure from the company. Usually, your boss will let the executives know as well as determine the appropriate time for a general staff announcement... follow their lead before sending out notifications to external contacts.

You should also ask your boss who will be handling inquiries or project details after you leave. This will allow you to inform anyone you are working with outside of the company about the personnel change and redirect them to the appropriate contact to avoid disruption or confusion.

Finally, set up an out-of-office auto-responder message on your company email address letting everyone know who to contact after you have left.

- **Documentation.**

Excellent employees who have the time to do so create a final checklist of upcoming project timelines and priorities that they hand to their employer on the last day. That way, the supervisor has a good read on what they need to hand off to other staff to keep the momentum going and not interrupt any programs that you had been working on.

Include details about key dates, project stakeholders, contact information, and tasks that need to be completed. Any boss will be grateful that you took the time to do this for them versus trying to bumble their way through unfamiliar projects!

- **Organization.**

Pull critical files and materials together so they are easily accessible as well as organize anything else relevant to the operation of your position. If someone can take the checklist and walk into your office and find all the associated information within reach, it makes the whole transition process much easier for everyone. An employer's worst fear is discovering a completely indecipherable mess on their hands left in the wake of a former employee.

- **Wrap up your benefits.**

If you have a balance of vacation time remaining, determine how that may be used or cashed out. Additionally, figure out how the new company handles health insurance… you may need to get a 30- or 90-day bridge with your old employer to cover the probation period at the new company. Also, you should determine how you want any retirement or pension funds to be handled. Inform your employer where you would like your final paycheck sent, or whether the employer will be handing it to you on your last day.

Follow up on outstanding expense reports or funds owed you. Conversely, if you owe the company any money, you should make immediate plans to pay it back so on your last day, the balance is zero for all parties.

- **Return all company property.**
If you have a company-owned laptop, make sure that no personal information (including emails) are on it. Hopefully, you never used it for personal use, and any logins to social sites have deleted passwords and cleaned out browser histories.

Make sure to have all keys, credit cards, cell phones, pagers, and any other company property is pooled together and ready to hand over. You don't want to keep making return trips to the company after you've already left.

Be aware that once you've given notice, the employer can choose to ask you to not come in at any point and also cut off access to email and voicemail by changing passwords, so you need to be mentally prepared to "cut the cord" the moment you have given notice.

Maintaining Your Brand Through Departure

Taking our cues (no matter how vicariously we lived through him) from former JetBlue flight attendant Steven Slater is *not* the blaze of glory that anyone should go out on, no matter how appealing that fantasy might be.

But any time we leave one company for another, there are sometimes hurt feelings no matter how delicately you try to smooth out the transition. Oftentimes, bosses feel "betrayed" that you are leaving the company, and this can lead to some pretty awkward and weird moments in the remaining time at the company.

Here are some ways you can maintain your professional brand for years to come.

- **Write a formal resignation letter.**

Even though you talked to your boss in person to give your notice, they might leave their job in the future. Instead, create something that outlasts their career at the company by writing a letter to be placed in your personnel file. Make it positive and personal to the supervisor. Outline how much you enjoyed your time at the company and maybe provide a couple of examples of amazing things you learned while on the job.

A formal resignation letter reinforces your professional polish and adds to your reputation as a classy person. *Never* write anything negative or vent. Remember, this letter can frame up the conditions under which you departed, and will be placed in your permanent personnel file. Be mindful of what will be in that file, should a future employer call your current company for references. When your file is retrieved, what will the human resources professional read about you?

- **Outline your accomplishments.**

Before you leave, create a report summarizing your positive contributions to the organization, and send it to your boss on or just before your last day.

By showing how much you achieved while there, this will leave a better taste in the mouth of the boss by reminding them that you were a good worker and brought something to the table. Who knows? There may be a future job opportunity at the company at a higher level that could prove to be your next career move, and having a favorable memory of your contributions could sway opinions in your favor.

- **Thank everyone.**

It's always a good idea to err on the side of being gracious (without being fake) – and thank your office mates. Be genuine, and let go of any hostilities that you may have held in the workplace.

Start off on a clean slate in your new job, and carrying around baggage from your previous employer doesn't do you any good. Let go, say thank you, then say good bye. It doesn't cost anything, and you might just surprise someone! And more importantly, you never know where you might run into them again, so the best way to go out is on a positive note.

- **Stay focused and don't "check" out.**

Bosses tend to understand that the excitement of an employee's new job can lead to certain "school's out for the summer" mentality, but you need to exceed those expectations to show that you are still committed to your current employer. Stay hungry, and keep putting in 100% so you are not perceived as a "short timer/slacker."

- **Tidy up loose ends.**

Finish up as many projects as possible, notify all stakeholders of a change in personnel and provide an interim point of contact. What you want to do is create a situation in which anyone could walk into your old job and be quickly up to speed on what projects are in the pipeline and which priorities need attention first.

"I Got A Job" Announcement

It's always amazing to hear about a friend or contact's job search, but then after awhile, they go completely silent. Only later do I find out that they actually landed a job and have been happily working for awhile.

What's wrong with this picture?

It is an amazing opportunity missed… the people that have been with you the whole way and cheering you along want to know that you finally landed somewhere. Why on earth wouldn't you make an announcement letting them know of the good news??

It's funny… we usually hear of people engaged in a job search because they are reaching out to their network, but most of the time, these same folks forget to tell their network when they actually land their next job.

Once you do find that next employer, be tactful in developing your message. It's important to always spin job announcements positively, especially when referencing previous employers. You never know where your message might land, especially if you are keeping in touch with anyone in the same "orbit" as your last company.

Example: "While I had a great run at _____ and learned a lot which enhanced my career, I am very excited to announce that I just have been hired on at _____ as their new _____."
This is a great way to get your network fired up about your success and also have set in their minds a sense of completion.

Everyone likes to hear good news, so why not share it? It is also another way to bolster your personal brand by showing that employers added you to their team as a valued team member.

This could also be a good time to throw a "thank you party" for everyone who helped you out during your job search. A simple, no-frills get-together at a local restaurant or at your house is a great way to celebrate and recognize those that went out of their way to assist you. This can serve as another positive boost to your personal brand while remembering them in your success.

Fitting Into A New Company

Just like breaking in a new car, there's that "honeymoon" period after you start your first day that requires extra special care and attention. You can't hit the gas too hard otherwise you risk spinning out of control and skidding out of the lines, even before you know where the lane markers are.

Smart career managers realize that it takes a delicate balance of assertively stepping up to job tasks and gaining the respect of co-workers and counterparts while carefully navigating around unknown landmines which could blow up right underneath their feet. Treading carefully and quietly is the savviest career move you can make as you get settled in.

While there is a lot of pressure for you cut the learning curve quickly to get up to speed, there are some important things to remember as you move into a new position.

- **Allow time for culture shock.**
It is one of the most unbalanced feelings to suddenly be thrust into a new work environment and have an unfamiliar routine to suddenly tame. There's the set-up phase which includes all the necessary paperwork and forms to get you into the company "system" and then getting your necessary business tools set up including your email address, passwords, and voicemail, as well as trying to make a mental map of the new office so you can find your way to the bathroom or break room without getting lost. Take this period one step at a time... it's bewildering, but you'll eventually build a routine that will put you at ease.

- **Keep your own counsel.**
Choose your words carefully and don't start sharing confidences until you have an accurate read on each person in your office. Sometimes the most "friendly" people in the office are actually outsiders looking to build an

alliance, and you could find yourself sitting on the wrong side of the fence without any understanding of the social or political implications of that friendship. Keep it professional and hold your cards close to your chest… it might take a while before you feel comfortable enough to trust co-workers.

- **Take time to get to know your boss.**

This person holds your career keys in their hands and it is imperative that you get on their good side from the get-go. The best way to find out what that good side entails is by getting to know them. I'm not saying that you need to get chummy, but making an effort to have lunch to ostensibly get up to speed could also serve as a rapport-building situation. Ultimately, you want your supervisor in your corner and to establish that they can trust you.

- **Hold off on the big ideas… for now.**

You may have proposed some grand ideas that caught the imagination of the hiring committee, but in reality, implementation usually requires a much longer lifecycle and integration process than just showing up on the first day of the job. Your goal is to study the organization and find the best way to integrate yourself into the company culture first. Once you are "plugged" in, then you can slowly introduce your ideas when the timing and opportunities present themselves. Otherwise, you might come in with too much too soon, and be perceived either as a threat to your immediate supervisor or to other co-workers.

COME UP WITH A FIRST-MONTH PLAN

Most companies have some kind of probationary period for new employees, but you should be thinking of this time as an opportunity to make yourself completely shine.

During the first week, take it easy in order to gain an understanding of tasks, learn people's names, and get the gist of the office layout. As details about your job duties become more clear, step into action.

Ask to meet with your boss and work together to develop some objectives that you both agree on to be completed within the first month of your hire. This will help you better understand the top priorities and also provide structure to your workday while you try to learn the ropes.

Do some pre-meeting prep work by evaluating any materials and notes left behind by your predecessor, so you can at least gauge what tools and information are available to help you do your job. Be sure to come up with a prioritized list of questions to ask that will give you the head start you need in the new job.

Next, identify key initiatives and provide action steps on how you plan to get up to speed with project stakeholders and priorities. Present concrete action items including scheduling one-on-one meetings with those people to build rapport and gain insight on details. Get your supervisor involved in what they see as top priorities and ask their opinion on specific areas.

Once you have a plan finalized, forward a completed version to your boss so they have a copy to follow along. This can be the document that you revisit when your probation period is up.

By developing this plan, you are actually seizing control of how your performance metrics will be measured and by working with your boss, you have just gotten their tacit buy-in that they agree to those terms.

SOCIAL MEDIA/INDUSTRY NETWORKING POLICIES

One of the things that can pose an immediate challenge to new hires is continuing the robust social media channel engagement and industry networking that has been built up during the job search. Given that you have gotten a full head of steam moving forward with building these channels, the last thing you want to do is cut the engine and kill your momentum.

Each company has a different policy on how they permit (or not) employee access to social networks during breaks. If this topic is not addressed during the new employee orientation process, you should ask what the policy is just to be clear on how the company views social media.

Some companies strongly encourage employees to participate in these platforms as part of their overall marketing strategy. By allowing employees to access social media, the employer is also tapping into each individual's network as part of a greater grassroots effort to build up the company image with people that might not have had contact with the company otherwise.

Other companies, however, have strict regulations about employee use of business resources for personal purposes and actually ban it. Many are concerned about falling productivity levels from employees that spend too much time online.

Another thing you should determine upon hire is the company policy for spending time out of the office at industry events and networking functions. Most employers "get" that this is an opportunity for their staff to make new contacts and potentially uncover new business prospects or ideas through networking.

Active career managers always make sure to factor having access to networking events in their daily job as a way to not only boost the company's profile within the target audiences but to also keep their own personal brand prominent.

WILDCARD: WHAT HAPPENS WHEN THE JOB I JUST TOOK TOTALLY BOMBS OUT?

For most of us, we accept new employment and never look back.

But for some employees, new ventures quickly dissolve into a nightmare shortly after hire, and their previous company starts looking pretty darned good all of a sudden.

So what exactly do you do when you are only a few short weeks or months into a new job, and it's not the right fit... or that it was the wrong decision?

This is a tough call. Staying in the wrong job could result in not performing up to expectations because your heart isn't in it. Or maybe the job was misrepresented during interview, and you find that you don't have the knowledge or expertise to execute.

<u>REAL-WORLD EXAMPLE</u>
I personally ran into this very situation. I was ready for change and had applied for and gotten hired on at another organization.

Three short months in, I was finding a disconnect between myself and the overall culture, made worse by a whole other component of my job duties requiring skills that I didn't even have... all of which had been greatly underplayed during the whole recruitment process by the new employer.

It was an agonizing decision.

I wasn't happy, and while I came into the office every day determined to do a good job, I felt that I was out of my league on this one facet of the job where I had no idea what I was doing. The whole situation was made even more difficult because a close industry colleague of mine had put his reputation on the line and recommended me to the executive.

If I left now, it would make everyone look bad.

Fortunately, I got lucky. I had stayed in touch with my supervisor from my previous employer (she was a mentor), and she made an offer for me to come back to the organization... the position I had left was still open, thankfully.

But I still had to give my notice to the new company after only 3 months.

So here's the letter that I wrote to my boss at the new organization:

"I am writing to you today to officially tender my resignation from (company name), effective (date).

I have found myself in a unique position that I have never before encountered. In the past three months, I have been very excited about the opportunity to step into the (position name) role at (company name) – especially with all of the amazing growth it has been experiencing in the past years. Add in the incredibly supportive board, enthusiastic members and super staff, and there is no doubt this is a winning team.

I have, however, been offered the position of (other position name) at (other company name), an opening in the industry where I have spent the majority of my career. It is an opportunity I cannot refuse.

Without a doubt, this has been, singularly, one of the most difficult decisions I have ever had to make. I have been torn between the two companies, as (company name) is poised to become an even greater success than it is already. I have been attracted to and excited by the tantalizing challenge (company name) poses: to carry it to that "next level." And yet, in spite of this wonderful challenge and opportunity, the offer from (other company name) has tugged at my heart strings. It's the industry with which I have had a 20-year love affair.

In being honest with myself and (company name), I have realized that the most competent leader is one who is an effective advocate in the areas where they have the most passion. While the good work of (company name) is in areas about which I care deeply, the passion I carry is for (industry name). Ultimately, this is why I have chosen to accept (other company name)'s offer.

(Supervisor name), I am sensitive to the fact that (company name) is just getting underway in expanding program capacities and I am willing to do anything in my power to assist in this transition, including assisting with initiating a search for my replacement and ensuring that program areas do not get disrupted as a result of my departure. You can count on my doing everything possible to make a smooth transition.

I am honored by the wonderful opportunity you have given me with (company name) and deeply moved by the amazing people I've met and worked with in the company. The support I have received during my time here is something I will always treasure.

Your leadership has taken the organization to new levels, and I am certain the new (position name) you select will help you take (company name) to the new successes you so clearly envision.

Thank you, again, for this opportunity to serve (company name). Please don't hesitate to ask any questions you may have."

And here's the personal note I wrote to the person who originally recommended me to the new job (as an apology):

"I truly owed you this letter as an explanation.

As you undoubtedly now already know, I gave my notice after three months of working at (company name) and am heading back to (previous company name) to a position there.

This decision to depart (company name) was probably the most difficult decision I have ever made in my professional career.

I realize that when leaders such as yourself gave your recommendation of me to (company name), this reflected on your impression of me professionally, and you put your reputation on the line. I want to thank you for that.

But more importantly, I owe you apology for not living out a full work span at (company name) that would've been expected, and had been implicitly suggested by your support of me.

During my short time at (company name), I was able to dive in and accomplish a great deal in a short period of time (to the expressed appreciation of the board). At the same time, however, I was being courted by (previous company) to return to the organization. But I felt as though I had already made a commitment to (company name), and would stand by it.

206

Nevertheless, I did receive an offer from (previous company name) that I could not resist, and finally accepted a position there.

I hope you can understand this journey I've undergone, and ask your forgiveness for not living up to your expectations and recommendations in the fullest extent."

In the bigger, long-term picture, if a job is simply not working out, the sooner you cut your losses, the better. As soon as things go south, this is when you need to get back on the job search saddle and start riding hard and fast towards the next stop.

From a résumé standpoint, remember, there is no "law" that states that you have to list every single job you've ever had... the résumé is what you volunteer about yourself. So if you have just a short stint at a company, don't feel like this will forever be an arrow in your side, twisting painfully. You can just write it off.

Of course, gaps in your work history or short-lived employment can and will come up in interviews. The trick is to address it directly by saying that it wasn't a culture fit and didn't work out. Then move on.

BOSSZILLA: SURVIVING THE WORLD'S WORST BOSS

What happens when you start a new job only to find out that your worst fears have come true? The person who is your supervisor is awful.

The cold, hard reality is: You are stuck.

Perhaps there aren't any potential job leads on the horizon...or maybe you don't have the financial resources or comfort zone to leave your current job. But there is that one thing that makes you dread heading into the office day after day to earn that paycheck: BossZilla is waiting for you.

Ever have the experience where your direct supervisor or organization leader is just The. Worst. Person. Ever? Many of us have. So what do you do? How do you make it work while you are trying to make your own ends meet?

Good question. Here are five tips for surviving on the job in what you might otherwise call "combat conditions."

- **Evaluate the costs of staying.**

Yes, if you are tight on money and this is your only income, this is a tough decision, but sometimes, when you start looking at the emotional or mental costs of what this bad boss is doing to you day in and day out, you might want to reconsider. Then there is the physical impact that a high-stress environment might have on you…and your family. While we normally always want to come out ahead, sometimes taking the loss and leaving a job to save our sanity and our health outweighs the paycheck. Only you can make that decision.

- **Grit your teeth and give them what they want.**

This takes a bit of swallowing one's pride, but we're talking survival here. Don't give in to your impulse to make a heroic stand. Instead, give them what they want. Think about means to the end in this situation. You need a paycheck and you do what is needed to get that paycheck. Never mind the other garbage in between. This is easier said than done, but keeping this mindset can help you make it through each day.

- **Go get counseling.**

Big surprise: Bad bosses are traumatic. The damage that they cause now can actually impact how you relate to others in the future by building up distrust and misgivings.

REAL-WORLD EXAMPLE

I once had a boss who sexually harassed me and was also extremely threatening and belligerent. When I finally mustered up the courage to get the heck out of that environment, I ended up withdrawn, scared, and very timid. It took months to come out of the very dark place to which I had retreated... counseling could have helped me keep my head above water in that situation.

Having a little extra help can also provide you with a better perspective so you can clear your mind of the poison being spewed by the boss.

- **Set the wheels in motion to get out.**

No one deserves to be berated, abused, or anything else that BossZilla can throw at you. Do an analysis of the situation. Sometimes, if there is a human resource manager available at your company, you can bring the bad boss issues to their attention, but there is always the risk that you could be terminated instead. The most important thing at this point is not to freeze like a deer in the headlights. Instead, a horrible boss and the company that retains people like that should act as a clarion call for you to keep things going swimmingly at your current position while you start throwing yourself into a concentrated effort to find alternative employment. Then get the heck out.

- **Excellence = Teflon.**

Your job isn't to make the boss look bad, but if you always excel in your work by being pleasant, having initiative, and doing good work, you may later end up earning compliments from your colleagues, co-workers, subordinates, and other industry partners. Not only is this a good way to build yourself a strong professional profile, but it can also deflect anything negative that BossZilla might say about you. In the end, they look small, angry, and ineffective.

Remember, trying to get the other person fired is a tough task and often backfires as BossZilla has likely laid traps for anyone who might try to go around them. Instead, it is always a good idea to document everything that this person does to you that are violations of office policies and procedures in case things really take a turn for the worse. That way, you can cover yourself while you are actively finding a way out of the organization.

STEPPING UP TO THE PLATE

After navigating your way through the learning curve of a new job, gaining comfort in your new role, and passing through the "honeymoon" phase, it's time to step up your game by building your reputation with your supervisor as an engaged employee eager to widen their contribution to the company.

A good way to score bonus points from the boss is to ask during a regular update session: "What areas are posing the biggest challenges for our department right now?"

Asking your supervisor about where help is needed can build your own organizational value by identifying areas where you can step up and accept more responsibility. This sends the right message to the supervisor that you are eager to contribute and thinking strategically about the operation as a whole by being willing to pick up slack.

But a word of warning: Only ask for and accept work that you can reasonably accommodate in addition to your existing duties. The last thing you want to have happen is fall into a situation where you get overwhelmed in an attempt to win over the boss, and fail in everything else. If this happens, it could backfire on your whole career if you can't complete the tasks for which you were hired.

CLOSE TO HOME   JOHN McPHERSON

"NO, we would NEVER ask an applicant for their Facebook info! We simply ask to implant a tiny computer chip at the base of your skull."

CREDIT: Special reprint permission from
John McPherson from "Close to Home" for use in this book

Keeping In Touch With Mentors

We've previously talked about how important mentors are in our job search. They are our base coaches, providing advice on potential moves or career decisions. They are sounding boards, cheerleaders, and advisors.

Keeping in touch with your mentors makes them feel good. By doing so, you express that you value them and what they have to say. But they also might provide counsel about areas that you might not have necessarily thought out. Or, mentors can provide insights on how to get out of tight jams.

Never forget that mentors oftentimes have experience and wisdom that eclipses our own. They've been down this road before and can offer you the support and counsel you need to have a rational voice in making key decisions in your career.

New Boss, New Strategy

Undoubtedly, most of us have gone through some kind of transition with our supervisors. Perhaps the person was recruited away to another company or maybe there was a merger and they got reassigned to another department.

Whatever the reason, something important has been lost. When your boss leaves, they take with them that person's knowledge of your contributions, skills, knowledge, and expertise.

And a new boss means a completely blank slate.

Your new job is to get to know them, ASAP. If you don't take the time to build rapport, it could have deadly consequences to your career.

The reason?

If they don't know your value, they could make decisions that don't factor you in as a valuable asset.

Try using these four tips to build a connection to a new boss.

- **Speak up in meetings.**
If you are always in the background, now is the time to jump in. If you aren't seen as an active participant on the team, this could be a red flag to a boss who might be surveying the landscape for potential house cleaning later. Be a positive and frequent contributor.

- **Set up a one-on-one meeting.**
If the boss has not done so already, set up a time to meet with them to provide an overview of your work and to allow them to get to know you better. Building connections will also help you both assess your working styles to figure out how you will be able to communicate best. This can lay the ground work for a great collaborative work relationship.

- **Provide regular updates.**
You don't need to be a classic "brown-noser" but proactively providing updates on project status or other work you are conducting is one less question or request that the boss has to make. If you reliably turn in work or reports on time and in an organized fashion, you'll be perceived as professional and as a model of efficiency.

- **Empower, Educate, and Engage.**
New bosses don't necessarily want to admit that they are behind the learning curve in getting acclimated to a new company or division. They are struggling to get caught up with priorities, challenges, and opportunities, while trying to get to know the team that will take them there. Be willing to share in a helpful way to give the new boss the knowledge

and tools to get them up to speed as soon as possible. You could gain a very powerful career advocate as a result.

If you build a reputation as a helpful, friendly resource who is competent in your work and an engaged member of the team, your new boss will see you as an important asset and include you in key projects and potential promotions.

Don't Fear The Hiring Anniversary – Harness It!

Most people heading towards the anniversary of their hire have some form of trepidation as performance review time nears.

But in active career management mode, employees should actually regard this benchmark as a positive time to discuss their accomplishments with their boss and use it as a great conversation about new opportunities to ensure continuous growth.

The most proactive way to handle this is to use the SWOT (Strength – Weakness – Opportunity – Threat) analysis for yourself and your work. This is an incredible tool for you to taken into the annual review session. For the most part, supervisors aren't very well-organized and haven't spent a lot of time parsing out the finer points of your job performance.

This is where you come in. Regardless of whether the employer has an "official" company personnel review form or not, if you take a proactive measure by developing a report that you hand to your boss, this can spark a dialogue and potentially open up new doors for you to grow professionally. It could also be a forum to discuss long-standing issues to collaboratively problem-solve the situation to identify solutions.

Either way, you come across as proactive, positive, solution-oriented, and caring about your job performance.

By developing your own SWOT analysis plan for the year, you are adding an element of accountability and also identifying things that could be out of your control that are impacting your ability to do your job.

In short, this is a brilliant solution to framing up the year in a manner in which you drive the conversation in an unthreatening way. Employers are very receptive to these discussions as you are demonstrating that you see the situation from their perspective.

Here's how to develop the SWOT analysis that can make a big difference in the coming year.

PERSONAL SWOT ANALYSIS FOR ANNUAL REVIEWS

Strengths: Provide bullet points about where you think you have truly excelled in the past year. This section is more skill-oriented: "Developed stronger business partnerships with key industry allies."

Sub-section: Below your strengths, bullet out the details of your top achievements in those particular skill set areas: "Forged partnership with ABC company which delivered $5 million in new revenues and increased company exposure on social media channels by 500%."

Weaknesses: Be careful writing this section, because you don't want to provide an employer with any negative ammunition and literally put a target on your forehead by offering up bad things you did. Instead, take this opportunity to redirect this section into positive territory that benefits the employer: "I felt that in the past year, I could use additional training in ABC skill set."

Sub-section: Provide a solution to shore up the weakness that you presented: "In the coming year, I would like to take an additional class to strengthen up that skill because I think this would be of benefit to the company by _____."

Opportunities: You are the ground-level expert in your job. Supervisors are too busy managing the big picture that they often miss identifying opportunities that subordinates see at the hands-on level. If you see something that might be of benefit to the company, start formulating a short summary and do as much investigation as you can on the potential impact it could have on the company. "I see an opportunity in the coming year to reach out to ABC previously untapped direction. Based on our new product models coming out in the next year, I think that by establishing a relationship with key influencers in this field, this could end up yielding $_____ in additional revenues to the company."

If the supervisor hasn't thought of this before, they will be grateful for your insight and ability to put the company first.

Threats:　　　　　　　Similar to opportunities, if you are watching trends and competitors, you can identify upcoming problems that might have blindsided the company otherwise. "In talking to one of our customers, I learned that our competitor is planning on revamping their product to gain an edge on our line... this could potentially take a big bite out of our business as a result."

At the end of your SWOT analysis plan, create a final summary of suggested action items that you think would be helpful to the company. Try to quantify everything as much as possible with numbers and do the research to know what costs might run. This will help the boss make a better informed decision about whether to proceed. By taking the step to provide this information proactively, this makes the supervisor's decision easier and less difficult to implement.

Additionally, having a detailed action list will provide you a final area of discussion during your annual review, rather than listing all the SWOT items and not following through with clear next steps.

Don't let this opportunity turn into a copy of your SWOT analysis lying on the boss' desk dying a slow death from neglect. The time for action is now, and if you can guide the discussion with proposed action items to be decided upon, you'll be more likely to spark action on the side of your boss.

8

Shaping Your Destiny

Knowing The Control Points Of Career Management

**"Watch your thoughts, for they become words.
Watch your words, for they become actions.
Watch your actions, for they become habits.
Watch your habits, for they become character.
Watch your character, for it becomes your destiny."
-Author unknown**

Every moment that we are in the workplace, what we do and say defines our destiny. How we say it, how it is delivered, and the intent behind it can completely impact how others see us.

Taking care in honing your communications skills is an area that requires constant monitoring and continuous vigilance for potential improvement. The best respected leaders are ones who make everyone feel important and valued. Why not follow that model?

Think about how you treat colleagues… if you remove the traditional hierarchical communications structure and treat subordinates as equals, chances are you will earn their respect. That's really what it is all about. How do you make others around you feel respected as valuable members on a team?

When I was younger, I was a very driven, Type A person who was fanatical about attaining perfection in everything I did. Of course, we all want to do a good job, but my mistake was that I judged others around me harshly if they didn't measure up to my standard.

One of my supervisors finally pulled me aside and opened my eyes and mind to the possibility of pursuing excellence instead… since perfection is an ever-elusive, unattainable goal. Her words of encouragement in shifting my thinking completely changed my outlook and enabled me to relax this rigid standard I'd been holding onto tightly. I still aim high but realize now that excellence is the only goal that is reasonable that any of us can attain. It was an amazing thought shift.

Interestingly enough, after I toned down my focus, I noticed that co-workers were much more receptive to what I had to say… and even more supportive.

The quote listed at the beginning of this section is one I saw many years ago and clipped out of a magazine. I actually had it laminated and now keep it on my desk as a daily reminder of how everything we do impacts our career destiny.

Pay attention to feedback and non-verbal clues to how people are reacting to you in an office setting. Do people seem eager and interested to hear what you have to say? Or do they barely acknowledge you and possibly dismiss everything you offer as irrelevant? It could be that your inner thoughts are coming out on your sleeve for everyone to see.

Practice thinking positively. If the work environment is toxic, work out your frustrations outside of the office by doing something productive like going to the gym. Find your fulfillment elsewhere so you can maintain your "game face" where it counts at the office. Keeping your career ship afloat and navigating through rough waters is your main objective, so don't get sucked into the emotional toxicity.

You'll need to be positive, interested, productive, engaging, thoughtful, polished, empathetic, patient, attentive, solution-oriented, and always think about the Golden Rule: "Do unto others as you would have others do unto you."

Another thought about how what you do and say impacts what others think of you: A growing problem that I am seeing is how poorly people write. Outgoing emails and correspondence are full of spelling, grammar, usage, and capitalization errors.

How you compose your communications also has an effect on your image. Yes, we all make mistakes from time to time (remember, excellence, not perfection), but if it is a consistent problem, that sends the wrong message to recipients who could include bosses or potentially a future potential employer. It connotes sloppiness, lack of concern, poor quality judgment, and disregard for others by not carefully composing a well-written communiqué.

Watch your thoughts and guard against being sloppy. Be as polished and professional as possible!

Thinking And Planning Proactively

Now that you are a proactive career manager, you'll be thinking and planning proactively about the key control points that impact your career destiny. You will need to think ahead versus waiting until the last minute and scrambling.

Every day, you need to take a moment and think about what you are doing that ties back into the bigger picture of your career. Ask yourself: Does the outcome of what I am currently working on have relevance to my overall career goals?

You'll need to think about keeping your career tools up to date, planning out professional development, joining industry organizations, mentoring others, and creating an overall career management file to manage it all. The next sections will provide you with information on exactly how to go about acting on these points.

Always Have A Contingency Plan

We all like to think that everything is just hunky-dory at our employer, but unanticipated changes can happen. Perhaps the company is sold. Maybe it goes out of business. Or management decides to clean house. If you are suddenly asked to provide details about your work, it could be that you are under intense scrutiny for a possible termination. Maybe a staff member has a vendetta against you. Or even financial conditions end up forcing staff cutbacks. Or the worst: you just plain screwed up. Whatever the reason, things can happen suddenly and without warning, and now you are being escorted out of the building, out of a job.

So what are you doing to prepare for the unthinkable?

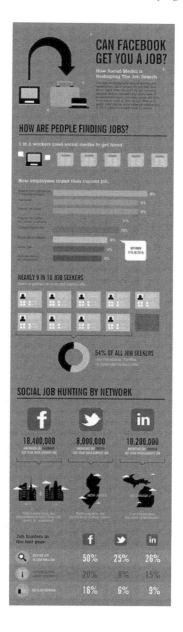

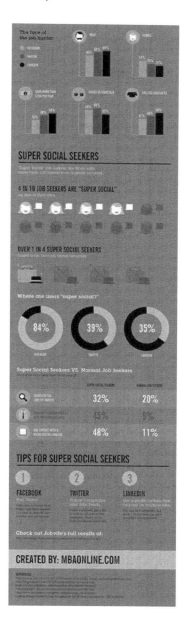

Credit: MBAOnline

You need to have a contingency plan in place and think out the steps you will need to take if this happens.

"Disaster planning" is serious business. But people rarely do it. They are more likely to come up with a fire escape plan from their home than to do any kind of advanced planning of job-loss scenarios, and even those are grossly neglected by the majority of the population.

By coming up with a plan that is "at the ready," you have just given yourself the best insurance policy possible. Of course, depending on your circumstances, you might get some kind of separation agreement or severance package. Or unemployment. But don't hedge all of your bets on those potential options. You need to be ready to depend on yourself first.

Below are some ways to build a contingency plan, which should be combined with the tactics described in the final chapter on managing one's career as a whole.

- **Build a financial cushion.**
Conventional wisdom and financial experts maintain that you should always have 6 months of living expenses in a savings account at all times for emergency purposes. The reality is that this protects you from being financially ruined should you lose your job. If you can manage it, you should aim for one year total. With many people going without work for 1+ years, it may take longer than you think to find your next job. Building a cushion will bring peace of mind knowing that you can make it for an extended period of unemployment without losing your home or car, let alone putting food on the table.

- **Know your career options.**
You should tier your career options in terms of short-term, emergency jobs versus long-term, career-related employment. Sometimes, the

urgency of the situation requires you to find work quickly and be less picky about the exact kind of job. Whatever you do, you should try to make sure that you align this "quick fix" job as closely to your long-term goals, but sometimes, this just simply isn't possible. If you have some luxury of time (from a severance package, for example), you can afford to be more methodical and tactical of the types of jobs you are going to focus on during your search. But understanding the two types of job searches is paramount to keeping your overall career focus at the forefront.

- **Diversify your income.**

Identify other areas where you might possibly generate income in the event of a sudden job loss, including consulting or leveraging other skills (perhaps not in your current job area) into other more temporary work. If you know what your options are and are prepared to act on them quickly, you'll feel much more reassured because you will have thought them out proactively rather than working in panic mode.

- **Pay attention to key indicators.**

Staying aware of what is going on at the corporate level or in the executive office can provide hints about potential changes. You need to be alert to financial statements, a whole slew of sudden closed-door meetings with senior management, company reports, and news reports. Sometimes, the signs were there all along but employees just didn't pick up on them, only to be stunned with business closures or massive office layoffs. Being forewarned is being forearmed. The sooner you can get advanced notice, the better of a head start you'll give yourself in the job search. *Always* pay attention to your gut instinct. It's more in tune with what's going on than you think!

- **Consider investing in protection insurance.**

The are some premium insurance products available that provide for a modest stipend or cover specific things like mortgages or "forgiveness" periods during job loss. Be prepared to pay top dollar, but they could be just the relief you need while you get your job search underway.

▪ **Understand your legal rights.**

Review what government benefits you could receive if you are let go from an employer. Did the employer violate any laws? Are you titled to unemployment insurance? If you are unsure, check with your local employment department to find out about what resources are available to you. If the matter has legal ramifications, contact an attorney who specializes in labor law for a definitive answer.

▪ **Identify and fill skill gaps as quickly as possible.**

Sometimes, we are so caught up in everyday work that the knowledge gaps we know exist simply never get filled because we don't have time to take the class. Knowing precisely where you might need to spend some time backfilling knowledge will help you be as competitive as possible upon launching a job search.

▪ **Ensure your career materials are ready to go.**

Being ready to immediately launch a job search without the delay of taking time out to update materials will put you considerably further ahead in the ball game.

Updating Your Career Tools

This point deserves its own section.

Why?

Most people do a terrible job of keeping their materials current. Think about the last time you updated your résumé… chances are that it was only when you had a job lead and had to pull everything together as part of the application process. Remember that panicky feeling?

But imagine how you would feel if you already had the document updated on a regular basis... instead of running around like the proverbial chicken with its head cut off, you smoothly and calmly take a quick look at it for minor last-minute tweaks, then send it off right away, versus embarking in a very stressful, hours-long and pressure-induced session.

Usually, when you are in that kind of a rush, you aren't quite confident that you remembered to include everything you needed to in order to make the application deadline.

Exactly.

So be proactive about updating career tools.

When I speak to groups, I make them take the Oath of Résumé Updates:

"I solemnly swear that I will update my résumé every 3-6 months because I know and understand that by doing so, I am prepared for any opportunities that present themselves or will save myself angst and actually be ahead of the game if I find myself in the middle of an unplanned job transition."

Whew.

That's a big thought but can be a life-saver. What you do now can be something you are extremely thankful for in the future. Think about how much time you will save by being nearly immediately ready to respond and how much more quickly you can enter the job search if you are already prepped and ready to go.

Another consideration to keep in mind when updating your career materials is to think about how your career might be evolving. Does your cover letter still reflect language that is from a lower position than where you are now? What kinds of skills can you add since your latest employment to make it more robust? Have you updated all your other social media outlets so there is consistency across the board? Does your LinkedIn profile match your résumé?

Constantly maintaining consistency on all of your career tools will be easier because you will only be making small tweaks across all channels versus a major labor-intensive update for all of them.

CREATING A CAREER MANAGEMENT FILE

I highly recommend creating a specific file where you can record all of your client kudos letters, supervisor compliments, classes that you take, organizations that you join, articles you have written, places where you have been featured or quoted, any materials that highlight you as a presenter, and any relevant career recognition (including awards, certificates, letters of appreciation, etc.).

It's pretty easy, and will help you recall details the next time you update your résumé by having all of this information at your fingertips. For example, as soon as you sign up for a class, print an extra copy of your registration and put it in this file. Same goes for membership dues payments.

Another type of documentation to keep on hand is your actual on-the-job performance. Since so many companies are operating lean and mean, most workers are running full-tilt from project-to-project, without any time to contemplate end results.

In just a few short years, the past becomes incredibly fuzzy as details fade from memory.

To solve this problem, make copies of your performance evaluations, staff reports, company reports and any other updates that contain information about the projects on which you've been working. Having this information to parse through when it comes to updating your career tools will be a godsend as well as a treasure trove, to help jog your memory.

Being an effective career manager means that anytime you run across any documentation that would be helpful to your career, you'll be putting it in this file for future reference. You'll be glad you did instead of trying to desperately recall blurry details from years past.

PROFESSIONAL DEVELOPMENT

There are three main drivers that can directly impact your career destiny that you can easily manage. Professional development, as discussed previously, is one of them. Anyone currently in the workforce, no matter what their career level, needs to consciously think about actively managing their own professional development.

This means that if an employer will not cover the expense of attending conferences or pay for certifications, you must step up to take care of it yourself. Are you really going to let a $200 class stand between you and your dream job? It is a minimal investment that can help set you apart from other candidates competing for the same job openings.

Employers are hiring actively engaged subject matter experts. You must continuously add to this knowledge base. And how you do this is by actively planning this out every year... until you retire.

Make a plan to add professional development goals as part of your annual New Year's resolutions... these are actually specific, accomplishable goals that can come in the form of a seminar, workshop, training, class, industry certification, webinar, conference, convention, tradeshow, corporate learning university, or any other similar type of sessions.

Be sure to keep track of all the information about the professional development programs you sign up for including the actual session title, sponsoring organization name, city/state (or online) where you took it, and the year that the session you attended took place. (You don't need to include the month or day.) The reason is that you add more credibility to your career tools when you can provide specifics.

Instead of: "Took classes in leadership."

It sounds a lot better to report:

"Leadership Training for Managers," Dale Carnegie Training – Atlanta, GA (2012)

Believe it or not, many people are that vague in reporting any job-specific training which is a missed opportunity to add the weight of a nationally- or industry-recognized training program to your career credentials.

Be specific and detailed in the programs that you have taken. But be aware that if you are self-taught (many people are), it is unusual and non-standard to include any books or publications that you read… you can save that discussion point for the interview instead. And this would be a good time to focus your efforts on identifying some outside professional development programs to sign up for in the coming year.

Mentor Others

Freshly minted and full of idealism, new grads are breaking into the toughest job market in recent history—which may be a challenge for them, but it's an opportunity for you.

Proactive career managers give back. Be a good leader and prepare these young professionals for a future in your industry, mentor new graduates, give informational interviews, and offer job advice.

Good leaders have succession plans. They take time to mentor subordinates. Instead of fearing younger, cheaper workers, proactive career managers consider the future—and the need for skilled labor moving forward. After all, it doesn't cost anything. Here are six ways you can influence the industry of tomorrow by working with the novice of today.

- **Speak at local schools.**

As a guest presenter, you are the face of your particular industry. You can inspire today's students to be tomorrow's leaders. Give advice, career tips and insights on lessons learned. You'll be surprised how many students listen.

- **Create a job shadow experience.**

Many schools have job shadow days. Invite a student to follow you around for a day, provide unique exposure to your specific sector and positively affect student job choices.

- **Set up an internship.**

An extra pair of hands can lighten the workload if you're running lean due to staff cutbacks. Offer a stipend to make the internship much more attractive. Students will be grateful for the opportunity to sharpen their skills while gaining valuable work experience.

- **Participate in informational interviews.**

As you advance your own career, you may come up in conversation as someone to "go talk to." Don't be surprised when you receive inquiring emails or phone calls from new graduates or current students. Take the time to meet. Remember, leaders are experts who share generously, and by being helpful and resourceful, you will solidify your reputation as exactly that.

- **Offer to be a resource.**

Too often, we graduate and move on, forgetting that we could be an invaluable resource to those who follow in our footsteps. Oftentimes, career centers and alumni departments struggle with connecting new graduates or current students with alumni who can act as amazing career bridges.

- **Mentor.**

I formerly taught at a community college as adjunct faculty. One of the students approached me looking for career advice. I helped brush up her résumé and connected her to some internships. Another industry colleague who also was teaching this student and I decided to split the cost and bought this person an industry membership, and she flourished. It was an incredibly rewarding experience for all of us to see her grow so quickly.

We can guide the future workforce by taking an active role in the careers of our youth and ensuring that our company and industries are passed into capable hands.

AFFILIATIONS

Affiliations are your memberships. Strategically joining industry-related organizations goes beyond just paying dues. This is your opportunity to buy access to the very people with whom you want to be associated. Most networking takes place within these settings so you should tactically think about which organizations would be most beneficial to you in terms of the quality of the membership.

Take the time to do your due diligence about potential organizations to join. You should take the time to attend a few meetings to get a feel for the culture and integrity of the association. Most will allow prospective members to attend a couple of meetings without being asked to join. This is your opportunity to conduct "reconnaissance" on whether investing in membership would be the right decision or not.

Actively managing memberships requires going beyond just writing a membership check. Many people have the mistaken idea that once you join an organization, all they have to do is sit back to realize the benefits of membership. However, it doesn't work that way. The best way to get the optimum return on investment for the membership dollar is to put effort into your membership.

That means attending meetings and getting engaged in the organization through volunteer engagements.

The rewards that you will reap will include access to the hidden job market. If you are involved in the organization and at the next meeting, you hear that one of your connections has left their job to take a position elsewhere, you have just heard, via word of mouth, of a hidden job opening before it is even posted. As a result, you have some time to network your way towards that job and hopefully arrive on the doorstep before any other job seekers.

Additionally, becoming a member of a professional industry organization is also a way to boost your personal brand while making yourself a known quantity. As a long-time member of Meeting Professionals International, I have made incredible contacts while at the same time cementing solid friendships based on mutual affinity and respect. This is how you boost your own profile within your peer group, which can make a difference in a job search whether you are currently employed or not working.

If you come to think of joining membership organizations as connecting to your particular industry's hub, you'll realize the importance of an investment in membership. The key is that if you aren't present, you won't have a chance once opportunities do become available because someone else is already ahead of you!

INVOLVEMENT

Beyond just joining an industry group, involvement means how you demonstrate your leadership and also your capacity to give back as a volunteer. Actively serving on committees and boards are great ways to step up your profile as a leader while finding an opportunity to work closely with others outside of your workplace. This can prove especially helpful to people just entering the workforce or if you are switching career fields into a completely new discipline.

In the past, I had been involved in tourism which meant working with travel agents, tour operators, and travel trade media. Which are all different "animals" from meeting planners. When I stepped into a new role of planning events, I joined the top meeting industry organization which was rather intimidating at first. But the walls quickly came down as I volunteered on the Membership Committee, which put me in touch with a small core working group on a monthly basis.

Volunteering enabled me to build rapport with industry peers outside of my own office… other people got to see my work ethic and personal brand in action, and I got to know theirs as well. By volunteering and working on a close-knit committee, I forged strong personal connections that last even today… and it's been 10+ years.

You can use involvement to gain new skills, expertise, access to otherwise non-public information, and leverage that for your career while giving back. This is a great way to manage your career, especially externally.

NETWORKING

Networking past your job search means maintaining contact after hire. Don't go radio silent once you land a new job... the worst career-killing move you could make is to ignore all the great people you've met and been cultivating as part of your new network. The art of networking means that you keep this process in motion *continuously* throughout your career, not just when you need a job.

More importantly, master networkers take the opportunity to transform new contacts into meaningful relationships.

Good networkers are comfortable with themselves, give generously, and have a clear idea of their goals. You should always have an idea of why you are at a meeting... what is your goal by attending a networking event? Be specific. "I would like to meet someone who has a contact at ABC company" is a specific networking goal.

Be advised that proactive networking is a delicate balancing act. Assertive networking is when you pace yourself but plan out your actions purposefully to lead to the right situations becoming available. The flip side is aggressive networking, where someone tries to force the issue in order to get what they want.

Always keep growing your network. You are building a giant farm where you are cultivating opportunities for future harvests.

Networking is all about exploring channels, leaving doors open, helping others, nurturing genuine relationships, and say YES to everything. You never know where these connections may lead!

CLOSING THOUGHTS

You and you alone are the sole driver of your career destiny. You cannot rely on a sense of job security because that simply doesn't exist anymore. Employees are not loyal to companies as they are either restless or craving more responsibility, or they are jumping ship for a better opportunity. Conversely, employers simply are not loyal to employees anymore because they are busy watching the bottom line.

Your employment at a company really comes down to being a business decision that you and the business both agree to. Being lulled into a sense of security by the family-like feeling of camaraderie is a dangerous place to be in... there are a myriad of reasons why an employer might cut you loose... from budget cutbacks to desiring new "blood" or for political reasons. The owner or management, no matter how much they like you, is in business, and their decisions are always going to put the company first and employees second.

What matters now is that you absolutely must start thinking in terms of how you are keeping yourself employable. Employers hire/retain highly skilled, knowledgeable, and productive workers, and tend to cut those who aren't about being a value-add to the current company... be *indispensable*. The job may be eliminated, but make sure you won't be!

And if you don't take control of your career management, you'll get left behind.

Career Management is:

- ✓ A dynamic, fluid experience and mindset.
- ✓ Not about picking one thing to do for the rest of our lives.

It is all about meeting change head-on, so we can respond nimbly to new opportunities or future job transitions that we can't control.

It is my hope that this book has helped wake all job seekers up as to what we need to be doing and when we need to be doing it so we can more effectively control our career destinies.

I want to share a closing thought with you which was a phenomenal post from Jason Alba, founder of JibberJobber.com. Jason is a top thought leader and captured the concept of career management so clearly that I asked him if I could reprint this word-for-word:

Job Search vs. Career Management – by Jason Alba

Job Search: I will start to look when I need to (unemployed, completely fed up, can see the writing on the wall, etc.).
Career Management: I am always in career management mode - I regularly do things that I need to in order to navigate quickly (and be in control of) future job transitions.

Job Search: I network to find immediate job opportunities, and hope that my network isn't too stale. (Or… "What network??")
Career Management: I have a very strong set of relationships and continually strive to add value to people who are in different circles than I am in.

Job Search: I find networking to be frustrating and non-beneficial to my search (and it takes too much time).
Career Management: As I nurture various relationships, I find great satisfaction in watching my contacts succeed, congratulating them when I can and offering to help as appropriate.

Job Search: I don't have time to volunteer… I'm too busy looking for a job.
Career Management: I actively volunteer in areas where I can contribute considerably to an organization and where I will meet other professionals that I want to get to know better.

Job Search: I have spent considerable time on my résumés and have "the perfect résumé." I hope I don't have to do this again anytime soon because it took a long time to tweak it just right.
Career Management: I keep a job diary.

Job Search: I share my personal brand through my résumé, interviews and my business cards I just got "for free" from VistaPrint.com. (Hint: Um, it is not exactly free.)
Career Management: I know what my value proposition is and I find ways to share this in various mediums. I have various elevator pitches (for different events), I know what a Google search on my name will produce, I have (or will have) some kind of strong presence online. Additionally, I'm buying a URL with my name and will start a blog once I figure it out.

Job Search: I don't have time to read one more article or book on the job search because it is time to find a job and I need to apply, apply, apply.
Career Management: I have a list of books (and other resources) that I read to help me understand my own career options including job search stuff (interviewing, résumés, etc.), personal branding, etc. I am not hurried through these books and mix in my own favorite reading, but make it a point to keep abreast on career issues.

Job Search: I hope my next job is at least as good as the last one (or way better).
Career Management: Each job change I have will (should) be a stepping stone to my ultimate career goals.

Job Search: I need something NOW (you know, mortgage, bills, mouths-to-feed, etc.) and am prepared to sacrifice what I really want to get what I need for now.

Career Management: My career is planned out - with flexibility. I won't have control over everything but I know that my career is mine to own, and I'm making sure that I do everything I can to work towards my end goals.

Job Search: I hate recruiters… Why don't they ever call me back?

Career Management: I have a handful of recruiters that regularly contact me. I'm interested in hearing what they have to say, and have no problem selectively opening my network to them.

Job Search: I can't wait until this is over so I don't have to do this job search stuff anymore!

Career Management: My career management is never over… it's a part of what I do.

Career management will overcome the lack of job security in today's economy by making sure you are as employable as possible, and open the doors to endless career possibilities.

And always remember as you go along your career path:

Be kind to everyone in your network and that you encounter. The universe is big… but it's a small world.

About The Author

Dawn Rasmussen, CMP, is a Certified Advanced Résumé Writer and the president of Portland, Ore.-based Pathfinder Writing and Career Services. Clients from across the United States and Canada and from all career levels have benefited from Dawn's highly-focused and results-oriented résumé, cover letter, and job search coaching services. Many professional groups as well as colleges and universities have appreciated the insights and expertise she shares during presentations on career management topics, and she is a frequently requested national speaker as a result. Dawn has also shared her knowledge as the official "Get the Job" columnist for *One+* magazine distributed to over 30,000 business professionals worldwide, and writes as a jobs expert for the "*Career Oxygen*" feature on Talentzoo.com, a job resource site for creative and marketing professionals. Recently, she has been featured in the *Chicago Tribune*, Careerbuilder.com, and *CBS MoneyWatch* as a career expert.

Additionally, she is a recognized career expert on Careerealism.com, which is a top 10 world-ranked career advice blog, and is a regular contributor to the weekly Hire Friday's #HFChat and TalentCulture.com's #Tchat meeting of the career industry minds on Twitter.

When Dawn isn't writing career documents, teaching, or speaking, she enjoys hiking in Oregon's spectacular outdoors with Brad, her husband, and their two dogs.

RECOMMENDED READING:

Bell, Greg. "Water The Bamboo," Three Star Publishing (2009).

Christen, Carol and Bolles, Richard N. "What color is Your Parachute? For Teens" 10 Speed Press (2010).

Crompton, Diane and Sautter, Ellen. "Find a Job Through Social Networking," 2nd Edition JIST Publishing (2011).

Doyle, Alison. "Job Search Guidebook," Alison Doyle Publishing (2011).

Hoffman, Reid. "The Start-up of You," Random House (2012).

Johnson, Tory. "Fired to Hired," Berkley Books (2009).

Kurth, Brian. "Test Drive Your Dream Job," Grand Central Publishing (2008).

Saltpeter, Miriam. "Social Networking for Career Success: Using Online Tools to Create a Personal Brand," LearningExpress LLC (2011).

Schawbel, Dan. "Me 2.0: 4 Steps to Building Your Future," Kaplan (2010).

Tyrell-Smith, Tim. "30 Ideas: The Ideas of Successful Job Search," Tim's Strategy (2008-2010).

Waldman, Joshua. "Job Searching with Social Media for Dummies," Wiley Publishing (2011).

Whitcomb, Susan Britton. "Résumé Magic – Trade Secrets of a Professional Résumé Writer," 4th Edition. JIST Publishing (2010).

Whitcomb, Susan Britton, Bryan, Chandlee, and Dib, Deb. "The Twitter Job Search Guide," JIST Publishing (2010).

Yate, Martin. "Knock 'Em Dead Résumés: Standout Advice from America's Leading Job Search Authority," 9th Edition. Adams Media (2010).

<u>Resources for hiring professional, certified résumé writers:</u>

Career Directors International
www.careerdirectorsinternational.com
The National Résumé Writers' Association
www.thenrwa.com
Professional Association of Résumé Writers and Career Coaches
www.parw.com

Stay Connected

Visit Our Website:

www.pathfindercareers.com

Receive free newsletter:

www.pathfindercareers.com

Twitter:

www.twitter.com/dawnrasmussen

Blog:

www.pathfindercareers.com/blog

Like us on Facebook:

www.facebook.com/pathfinderwritingandcareers

19391930R00146

Made in the USA
San Bernardino, CA
25 February 2015